SEMINAR STUDIES IN HISTORY

General Editor: Roger Lockyer

Philip II

Geoffrey Woodward

Head of History,
Wellington School

LONGMAN
London and New York

Longman Group Limited,
Longman House, Burnt Mill, Harlow,
Essex CM20 2JE, England and Associated Companies throughout the
world.

Published in the United States of America
by Longman Publishing., New York.

First published in 1992
Fourth impression 1995.

Set in 10/11 point Baskerville (Linotron)

Produced through Longman Malaysia, ETS

ISBN 0 582 07232 8

British Library Cataloguing in Publication Data
Woodward, Geoffrey
   Philip II. – (Seminar studies in history)
   I. Title   II. Series
   946.04092

ISBN 0-582-07232-8

Library of Congress Cataloging-in-Publication Data
Woodward, Geoffrey.
   Philip II/Geoffrey Woodward.
      p.   cm. – (Seminar studies in history)
   Includes bibliographical references and index.
   ISBN 0-582-07232-8
   1. Spain – History – Philip II, 1556–1598. 2. Philip II, King
of Spain, 1527–1598. I. Title. II. Series.
DP178.W66 1992
946'.043 – dc20
                                            91–29579
                                            CIP

Contents

Contents

A note on currency

In Philip's reign, accounts were kept in *maravedís* and *ducats*. Exchange rates fluctuated and values of currencies varied from decade to decade but the most common valuations and the ones used in this book are:

375 *maravedís* = 1 *ducat* = 6*s* 8*d* [33p]

Acknowledgements

To Clare, Susan and Helen

Cover: Peter Paul Reubens: *Philip II*, Prado, Madrid (Photo: Bridgeman Art Library)

Seminar Studies in History
Founding Editor: Patrick Richardson

Introduction

The Seminar Studies series was conceived by Patrick Richardson, whose experience of teaching history persuaded him of the need for something more substantial than a textbook chapter but less formidable than the specialised full-length academic work. He was also convinced that such studies, although limited in length, should provide an up-to-date and authoritative introduction to the topic under discussion as well as a selection of relevant documents and a comprehensive bibliography.

Patrick Richardson died in 1979, but by that time the Seminar Studies series was firmly established, and it continues to fulfil the role he intended for it. This book, like others in the series, is therefore a living tribute to a gifted and original teacher.

Note on the System of References:
A bold number in round brackets (**5**) in the text refers the reader to the corresponding entry in the Bibliography section at the end of the book. A bold number in square brackets, preceded by 'doc.' [**doc. 6**] refers the reader to the corresponding item in the section of Documents, which follows the main text. A word followed by an asterisk, for example, 'Inquisition*', indicates that the term is defined in the Glossary.

ROGER LOCKYER
General Editor

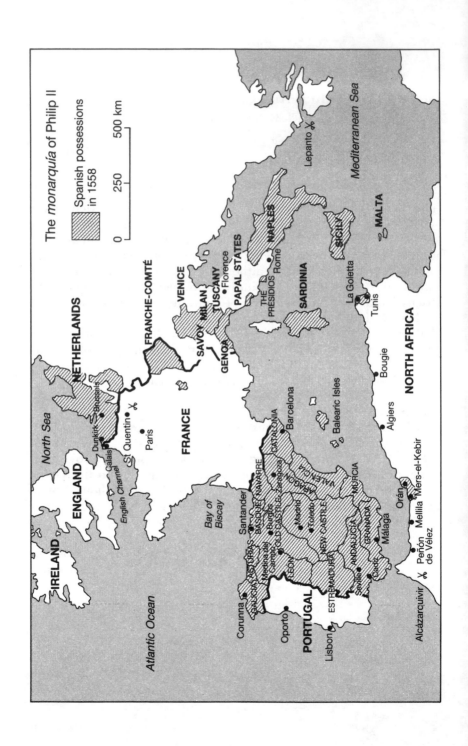

Part One: The Background

1 Charles V's Legacy

On 16 January 1556 Emperor Charles V abdicated as King of Spain and formally transferred the last of his possessions to his only son Philip. The inheritance was impressive by any standards. The Iberian kingdoms of Castile, Aragon, Catalonia, Valencia and Navarre had been brought together by the union of Isabella and Ferdinand, 'the Catholic Kings', and secured by their grandson Charles. In effect, Philip's Spain was a dynastic union rather than a unified country, a geographical expression rather than a nation state. Each dominion was autonomous and equal, distinguished by its own laws, language and customs, so that subjects identified themselves more readily with their *país** than with their monarch. Not until the 1590s did Castilians refer to the 'Spanish Empire'; even the term '*español*' was imported from Provence (**82**). National consciousness was slow to develop partly because Aragon was oriented more towards the Balearics, Sardinia, Sicily and Naples and the recently acquired Duchy of Milan, but also because Castile's mantle of imperialism stretched south and west towards North Africa, the Caribbean, and Central and South America. To these two areas of divergent interests a third had been added which altered the entire configuration of Habsburg Spain. In 1555 Charles transferred his Burgundian territories from the House of Austria to Philip and Spain (**40, 80, 153**). In reality Burgundy had little in common with the Spanish Habsburgs. Town councils, provincial assemblies and *stadholders** throughout the seventeen Dutch provinces had resisted earlier attempts by Charles to impose a more centralised administration. Only the nobility remained outwardly loyal, mainly because their Regent, Mary of Hungary, had had the good sense to include them in the Council of State and to respect their chivalric Order of the Golden Fleece (**61**). Unless it was carefully handled, Philip's Burgundian inheritance would prove more of a liability than an asset (see pp. 61–71).

Political and geographical disunity was, however, offset by a common strain of Catholicism which permeated the Spanish character and created a powerful spiritual bonding. Since the beginning of the

1

*Reconquista**, Christian Spaniards believed their destiny was to expel the Moors from the mainland and to purge Spain of this religious and cultural blight. It was the Most Catholic King's duty to defend the interests of God and His Church both in Spain and beyond, a responsibility which Charles had taken very seriously. He had encouraged the Inquisition* to arrest the growth of Illuminism* in the 1520s and Erasmianism* in the 1530s and, although there were isolated pockets of heresy discovered subsequently, his principal concern had been the external threat of the Turks and their suspected links with fifth-columnist Moriscos* in Spain. As the empires of Suleiman, the Turkish Sultan, and Charles expanded in the Mediterranean and Central Europe, clashes occurred at the periphery like the interaction of continental plates, but neither side was strong enough to inflict a decisive defeat. Charles's preoccupation with French and German problems in the 1550s, allied to his deteriorating health, saw the initiative pass to the Ottomans who seized Tripoli, Peñón de Vélez and Bougie. The Turkish threat to mainland Spain, her Mediterranean possessions and remaining outposts in North Africa was the most serious challenge facing Philip at his accession (**38**) (see pp. 77–80).

His greatest domestic problem in 1556 was financial, a direct legacy of the political and imperial achievements of the Catholic Kings and Charles V. In 1554 the Regent Joanna, Charles's sister, informed him that revenues had already been pledged for the next six years and she could not see how the administration could continue to support his wars. Two years later Philip inherited a state debt of some 36 million *ducats* and an annual deficit of 1 million *ducats*. In fact, Charles had financed his imperial commitments by a series of expedients without ever tackling the fundamental issues. The wealthiest sectors of society were exempt from paying direct taxation and the burden fell on the poorer groups. Although most ordinary revenue came from indirect taxation, the system was unequal and in need of reform; but the landed, clerical and merchant classes resisted any attempt to introduce new taxes or extend existing ones. Outside Castile, the provincial *Cortes** proved even more unwilling to defray the crown's costs, arguing that taxes should be spent where they were raised. Increasingly the Low Countries came to subsidise Charles's wars and in 1555 were supplying over 3 million *ducats* a year (**141**). Although there was some merit in Charles's claim that 'I cannot be sustained except by my realms of Spain', he meant in effect Castile and the Netherlands. Fortunately the volume of gold and silver from the Spanish Indies had also been steadily growing, but much of this money was already earmarked to pay off crown debts. Isabella and Ferdinand had introduced the practice of issuing *juros** (credit bonds) to bankers, thereby mortgaging future state income. By 1556, 68 per cent of ordinary revenue was consumed in servicing and repayment of these *juros*. Far worse was the practice of granting *asientos** (advanced contracts) to foreign and Spanish financiers whereby the crown received a loan in return for bills of exchange. *Asiento* repayments came to over 14 million *ducats* in 1556 and the *Cortes* regularly complained of the vice-like grip foreign bankers had on Spain's finances (**17**) (see pp. 33–8).

Charles introduced no fundamental changes to the financial administration but instead allowed the bureaucracy to multiply and the level of expenditure to increase accordingly. Admittedly he was not helped by the steady rise in inflation which saw prices in Spain double between 1500 and 1550, but his response was to raise direct and indirect taxation and resort to a variety of money-raising schemes. Crown land was leased at favourable terms, rents farmed out and land sold off, and public offices, privileges and monopolies granted to those who could pay. In this way many royal salt, silver and mercury mines had been privatised and the right to administer the land belonging to the *Maestrazgos** (Military Orders) had been granted to the Fuggers, the Augsburg bankers, in 1525 (**70**). Philip inherited many serious financial difficulties from his father and would have been well advised to apply Charles's advice: 'Attend closely to finances and learn to understand the problems involved.' Regrettably, neither Charles nor Philip paid much attention to this aphorism.

2 Philip II's Character

Philip was born in Valladolid on 21 May 1527, the eldest son of Charles V and Isabella of Portugal (see Genealogical Table, p. 114). In more ways than one he was the product of his parents: short in stature with an upright posture, his most striking features were his large blue eyes set in an egg-shell complexion, his reddish hair and his disproportionate upper jaw and lip [**doc. 1**]. He had neither a strong physique nor good health, and within twenty years his body had become rounded, his hair and beard turned white and his eyes were bloodshot with fatigue.

Philip's early education fell to Martínez Siliceo and Bartolomé de Carranza and a variety of specialist scholars. He soon developed a liking for mathematics and architecture but showed no flair for foreign languages and only felt comfortable when speaking Castilian, which partly explains his self-consciousness in the company of foreigners and his reluctance to travel outside Spain. Don Juan de Zúñiga was put in charge of physical activities, but it soon became clear that the prince much preferred walking, dancing, music, playing piquet, chess and reading books on natural history to robust activities. Philip was an aesthete, not an athlete. Charles recognised the value of Philip acquiring political experience as soon as possible: at the age of twelve he attended council meetings, at sixteen became Regent of Spain and in his twenties travelled to Milan, the Empire, the Netherlands and England. But it was not Philip's wish to be away from Spain. 'Travelling about one's kingdoms is neither useful nor decent,' he once informed his son, and after 1559 he never left the Iberian peninsula (**123**).

Philip's devotion to the Catholic faith owed much to his mother. Isabella of Portugal spent many hours each day in prayer, and in his infancy Philip was surrounded by clerics whom he was taught to revere. Throughout his life, he attended Mass daily, heard sermons weekly and received Communion quarterly. Pious and orthodox in his devotion to the Catholic Church, he endowed monasteries and shrines, kept religious books at his bedside and saw evidence of divine intervention in all affairs. God was omniscient; His cause was Philip's cause.

Traditionally, Philip has been seen as hostile to occult philosophy, yet recent research clearly contradicts this view. He is known to have acquired more than 200 books on magic, kept a horoscope prepared by Matthias Hacus, received frequent advice from astrologers, ordered all extant works by the medieval Majorcan philosopher Ramón Lull to be brought to the Escorial, and patronised alchemists like Diego de Santiago (**50, 136, 143**). Throughout his life he developed an interest in mathematics, science and technology. In 1583 he founded an Academy of Mathematics and Science and established four chairs under the directorship of Juan Herrera to educate Spanish students in military engineering, architecture, navigation and mathematics. He financed inventions such as Giacomo de Francisco's secret method of careening ships' bottoms and Antonio Marin's war machine which 'fires shot and darts with much impetus and effect, and without expense in powder or danger of fire' (**51**, p. 134). Philip's mind was never closed or narrow, and his thirst for knowledge was insatiable – particularly if it would give him a military advantage or benefit him personally.

From an early age he had been an avid collector of manuscripts, books and works of art. Pliny, Dante and Petrarch nestled alongside Aesop's *Fables* and writings by Erasmus and Teresa of Ávila. The Prado came to possess the paintings of Bosch, Brueghel and Titian whom he particularly liked, as well as the works of Spaniards like Pacheco and Coello whom he disliked (**4, 168**). At his death his palaces housed more than 700 paintings and the largest private library in Europe. Philip used his knowledge of architecture to design and oversee personally the building of several palaces. Each possessed a distinctive feature: at Casa de Campo, mock sea-battles were performed on artificial lakes and fountains; Aranjuez became the principal repository of thousands of varieties of trees, plants and herbs; Casa and Aranjuez housed elephants, rhinos and lions, and at El Bosque a royal game reserve was built to provide deer and pheasant for hunting. Undoubtedly the Escorial is the greatest monument to Philip's love of architecture, mathematics and spiritual devotion. It was designed by Bautista and completed by Herrera, and Philip chose its site 48 km from Madrid and 1,000 metres above sea level on the foothills of the Guadarramos (**86**). Part palace where Philip resided most spring and summer months from 1566, part mausoleum where he housed his dead relatives, and part Jeronimite monastery, the Escorial embodied Philip's temperament.

In it he was isolated from his councillors and subjects at large; it was his ultimate defence against an intrusive world. There amid the dark, narrow corridors and secret passages, in austere cells built of grey granite blocks, he occupied a small room overlooking the monastic church of San Lorenzo.

As the seasons changed so the court progressed from one palace to another, and if its ethos was not as lively and resplendent as under Charles, it was far from dull. Dancers, acrobats, buffoons and more than twenty dwarfs, including several from the Zaragoza lunatic asylum, entertained the royal household, and a particular favourite was the retarded Magdalena Ruiz who could be relied upon to act the fool. More serious entertainment was provided by the court composer Tomás Luis Vitoria, the organist Antonio de Cabezón and chorister Philippe Rogier, who together with 150 musicians fulfilled the King's love of music, even if he disdained the innovative musical chants of Palestrina in favour of traditional plainsong. Dramatists and writers like Lope de Vega, Lipsius, Montano and Velasco were patronised by the crown, and the poet Juan Rufo received a 500-*ducat* subsidy towards the cost of publishing his *Austriada*, an epic poem about the Habsburgs (**4**).

Philip's relationship with people was deceptive and has deceived many historians mainly because he developed an iron self-control to mask his feelings in public. Outwardly he appeared reserved and courteous, performing his daily routine in a grave and dignified manner. An arch-bureaucrat dedicated to the endless task of administrating his *monarquía**, he spent nine hours a day every day reading and annotating papers, listening to advice and taking decisions. Men who knew him, like Cardinal Granvelle, viewed him as a procrastinator and claimed that 'in all his affairs, his sole decision consisted in remaining eternally indecisive'. Although there is much truth in this remark, Professor Parker has reminded historians that Philip only appears hesitant and uncertain in times of crisis because a great amount of documentary evidence written by the King at such moments has survived (**123**). Given the changing nature of international affairs and the slowness of communications, it was often wiser to be cautious and prudent (**116, 117**). Yet once Philip had taken a decision he kept to it in an inflexible, determined manner. C. G. Bratli suggests that 'history should list this steadfastness of purpose – which people so often term intolerance and fanaticism – as the most striking quality of that King', but to Philip appearance was everything and a compromise or retraction was a sign of weakness even when he was wrong (**11**, p. 129). It is this juxtaposition of irresolution and constancy, of weak- and high-mindedness which makes him such a paradox (**36, 97**). Of course, he was not above deceit and could be as ruthless as the next prince, but to label him a 'systematic liar and hypocrite', 'the great father of lies who sat in the Escorial', as some historians have done, throws more light on them than on him (**118, 121**).

Philip's private life functioned around his public duties; the one rarely interrupted the other. At pre-determined times he was available for his family – at 10 a.m. before Mass, after dinner at 9 p.m. and just before bed – but for most of the day he was alone. 'Being by himself is his greatest pleasure,' commented the Venetian ambassador, who for once may have been right. The King regarded marriage as a dynastic and diplomatic obligation, but misfortune necessitated his marrying four times. Maria of Portugal (1543–45) died giving birth to Don Carlos; Mary Tudor (1554–58), with whom he spent seventeen months, died childless; Elizabeth of Valois (1560–68) produced two daughters, but the sudden death of the Queen and Don Carlos within ten weeks of each other obliged Philip to marry again. 'I very much desire to remain as I am,' he candidly informed his future mother-in-law, but his final marriage was a success: Anne of Austria (1570–80) provided him with five children, although only Don Philip survived puberty.

The King's relationship with his children has been the subject of much discussion even if too many historians have concentrated on the fate of his eldest son, Don Carlos, and too readily believed the allegations surrounding his death (**16, 118, 179**). William of Orange claimed in 1580 that the prince had been murdered, and Antonio Pérez – who was in a position to know, yet biased when he gave his version of events – confirmed in 1594 that he had been poisoned. Philip showed little love or affection for his psychotic son, whose manic outbursts convinced him that he must be placed under restraint. But if Carlos's subsequent treatment seems cold and heartless – he was kept in solitary confinement, his household disbanded, his name erased from all prayers; and when he died in July Philip did not attend the funeral – it does not follow that the King was responsible for his death or felt no grief. Nevertheless, it remains clear that Philip was far more attached to his two daughters, Isabella and Catalina, as his letters written whilst he was in Portugal demonstrate (**43**) [**doc. 2**]. In the 1580s he spent up to four hours each evening reading state papers to his eldest daughter, and his younger daughter received 127 letters when she moved to Savoy with her husband in 1585.

Philip could never be a popular king because he isolated himself from his subjects, restricted his appearances in public and, following two attacks on his life in the early 1580s, travelled in a sealed coach. Respected, feared but never loved by his people, he possessed many of the qualities that Spaniards admired and all that his enemies despised. To Castilians he was modest, pious, handsome, just, benevolent, absolute, 'El Prudente'. To his critics, he was arrogant, hypocritical, bigoted, sadistic and tyrannical, 'the spider King . . . the weaver of plots'.

Part Two: Descriptive Analysis

3 Government and Administration

The nature of Philip II's government

In an age of personal monarchy Philip II epitomised its strengths and weaknesses. More than any other European ruler he assumed total responsibility for governing his subjects and saw it as his duty to God to fulfil this obligation. The task he set himself was far greater than it needed to be but his devotion to the Catholic faith and obedience to his father's testament shaped the destiny of Spanish history.

In 1543 Charles V had exhorted his son to 'depend on no-one but yourself. Make sure of all but rely exclusively on none. In your perplexities trust always in your Maker. Have no care but for him' (**10**). Philip applied this advice with exactitude, developing an inveterate distrust for his ministers and never doubting that he alone should take all decisions in matters of government. A slow thinker and extremely cautious, Philip always preferred to administer by paper. It was, he contended, more discreet and secure than listening to suggestions, but it is more probable that he felt uneasy in councils, where he might have to make an instant decision. Everything and anything fell within his compass: from investigating the cost of soldiers' clothing in Brussels to determining the education of Mexican children, from allocating the sailors' berths on the Armada to processing applications for the export of Andalucian horses. Finding it nearly impossible to delegate, he lacked the political judgement to discriminate quickly between the important and the trivial. As the reign progressed so the volume of administration multiplied: in 1571 he was reading and annotating an average of forty memoranda a day, and on one occasion he read over 400 papers. Gradually his health began to give way. 'Those devils, my papers' were reportedly giving him severe headaches and eye-strain in the 1570s and at times he despaired how he could continue. In 1577 he told his secretary: 'I have just been given this other packet of papers from you. I have neither the time nor the strength to look at it, and so I will not open it until tomorrow. It is already past 10 o'clock and I have not yet dined' (**123**).

In addition to the daily routine, petitions and letters required answering. Administration was a time-consuming business and before any decisions were taken, many intermediaries were consulted, sometimes on several occasions, and secretaries spent hours with the King achieving the exact wording he required. The bureaucratic machinery turned over at its own measured pace. 'If death came from Spain, I should be immortal,' said Granvelle; Gonzalo Pérez expressed the same feeling more poignantly when he complained, 'Decisions are taken so slowly that even a cripple could keep up with them'. Part of the problem was the slow and uncertain communications. Philip's postal service, organised by Gabriel de Tassis, was one of the best in Europe: letters took four days to reach Madrid from Lisbon, ten from Brussels, fourteen from Milan and twenty-six from Rome, but adverse conditions caused delays and the inevitable result was frustration all round. Councillors, viceroys, governors and generals awaiting orders could only guess at the cause of delay, and by the time they had received a reply to an urgent request, the circumstances had changed and further instructions were required. Some councillors circumvented the long delay by taking decisions without obtaining royal assent, but this only added to the air of distrust, and once Philip suspected someone of subterfuge he set out to trap them by deliberate duplicity. It was apparent to Pérez as early as 1565 that 'His Majesty makes mistakes and will continue to make mistakes in many matters because he discusses them with different people, sometimes with one, sometimes with another, concealing something from one minister and revealing it to another' (**70**, p. 145). In the opinion of Professor Koenigsberger, the result was 'administrative chaos' in the Empire and political intrigue in Madrid (**83**, p. 81).

Philip was never short of advice. In fact, he probably received too much and could not readily digest it. Much of the routine administration was delegated to his more trustworthy officers, but ministries were short-lived and unsettled because he was eternally suspicious. One of the most spectacular dismissals was that of Cardinal Espinosa who, according to the King, was the ablest of all his servants but nevertheless fell from power when he assumed too much responsibility. His fall paved the way for Mateo Vázquez to rise to prominence as Philip's private secretary and confessor between 1573 and 1591, and he provided the continuity of government which factional rivalry and Philip's intriguing did so much to frustrate (**98**). Vázquez suggested that he should read the King's private correspondence, memorials and *consultas**, and then draft the appropriate recommendations which Philip would approve by initialling. Philip agreed and took his advice on many issues. It was probably Vázquez who urged him to adopt the *ad hoc* committees known as *juntas** in the 1580s as the best method of digesting advice. Only Vázquez knew the secret contents of each *consulta* and Philip only knew as much as he was told. Vázquez's long tenure in office owed much to his skill at playing down his own importance in the administration and not giving any cause to suspect or distrust him. It was a singular achievement.

Three consistent traits are apparent in Philip's administration. First, he generally preferred Castilians to all other subjects. Men like Espinosa, Ovando, Vázquez, Zúñiga and the Guzmán, Mendoza, Enríquez and Toledo families dominated central government, and only a few outside the charmed court circle received principal appointments and rewards. While it is true that advisers such as Gómez de Silva and Moura were Portuguese, Idiáquez a Basque, Requesens a Catalan, Granvelle a Franche-Comtois and Farnese an Italian, contemporary evidence suggests that appointments were biased and caused resentment. 'The Castilians want everything, and I suspect they will end up by losing everything,' confided Granvelle to Margaret of Parma.

Second, the King's desire to be well informed led to ministers attending several councils and *juntas*, whereby each acquired just enough knowledge to keep the others in check but never enough to be omnipotent. Francisco de Eraso was secretary to six councils and a member of two more in 1559, and Cardinal Espinosa served as President of the Councils of Castile and the Indies, and also as Inquisitor-General. Councils also regularly interfered in one another's domains: the Council of Finance audited other councils' accounts, the Council of the Inquisition interposed in the Council of Aragon's affairs, and the Council of State argued with the Council of Italy.

A third distinctive feature of Philip's central administration was the preponderance of legally trained bureaucrats, products of the expanding university system (**65**). These *letrados**, like the equivalent *officiers* in France, came increasingly from the middle and urban classes, and it was they who consistently occupied the principal administrative offices. All thirty-nine councillors appointed to the Council of the Indies, for instance, were trained in the law, and none of Philip's personal secretaries was of noble birth. Of course, as the administration expanded and Philip sought to increase state control, so he required more lawyers than grandees and nobles. As a result, personal quarrels between grandees and *letrados** were never far from the surface, and ministers, secretaries and officials were always ready to cut the ground from one another's feet.

Conciliar administration

Philip's decision in 1561 to establish his capital in Madrid rather than in Toledo or Valladolid ensured that he would be surrounded by his central councils which, by the end of his reign, numbered fourteen. Each exercised executive, legislative and judicial functions, and although Philip was kept informed on a daily basis, considerable power rested with each of the presidents and their secretaries. Despite its appearance of centralisation, the administration was really an *ad hoc* system of councils with the King at the centre. Six councils were territorial. The Council of Castile, the highest council in the realm, acted as the supreme court of law, dispensing justice, hearing appeals and making recommendations to the King. The Council of Aragon was the principal organ of communication between the King and Aragon, Catalonia, Valencia, the Balearic Isles and Sardinia. Acting as the supreme court of justice for all but Aragon and Catalonia, where the *audiencia* (appeal courts) heard cases, it also handled all Italian affairs, but from 1559 a new Council of Italy was set up to administer Naples, Sicily and Milan. This measure was disliked by the Aragonese, who correctly envisaged a reduction in their authority and patronage, and by the Italians, who were suspicious of all reforms from Madrid. Philip tried to reassure them by insisting that three of the six councillors would be Italian, but he nevertheless ensured that the principal offices of president and treasurer were reserved for Castilian nobles and prelates such as members of the Cabrera and Perrenot families. The Council of the Indies was responsible for the internal affairs of the New World which from 1580 included the ex-Portuguese territories. Staffed by jurists and theologians rather than by colonial experts, the council issued thousands of edicts to the viceroys in Mexico and Peru but exercised little real control over the government of the Indies and the welfare of the natives. Two new councils were created in the 1580s: the Council of Portugal in 1582, through which Philip corresponded with his viceroy in Lisbon, and in 1588 the Council of Flanders. Since 1559 Philip had administered the Netherlands and Franche-Comté through secretaries at the court in Madrid who corresponded with the governor-general and privy council in Brussels. The new Council of Flanders was designed to achieve greater efficiency and regularity of procedure but it is questionable how far royal administration was improved.

In addition to the territorial councils, there were eight departmental councils which dealt with particular aspects of government. The Council of the Inquisition was responsible for twenty-one tribunals throughout the *monarquia**, and its ability to interfere in secular matters in the name of religion made it a valuable pillar of the state. The Council of Military Orders was largely redundant in Philip's reign, as was the Council of the Crusade whose main function of administrating the *cruzada** had been taken over by the Council of Finance. Charles V had seen the wisdom of setting up a *Cámara* (or Chamber) to control patronage and royal appointments in Castile, which Philip reformed seventy years later, as well as a Council of State to supervise foreign affairs, a Council of War, a Council of Finance and a *Junta des Obras y Bosques* to administer royal buildings, gardens, lakes and forests. Philip made no attempt to unify these councils but instead treated them as separate satellites responding to his commands. In this way he hoped to know all aspects of a problem anywhere in his Empire at any given moment. In practice, however, his knowledge was fragmentary and at times inaccurate, and as he never travelled outside the peninsula after 1559, he had no ready way of validating what he had been told.

The Council of State

In so far as any one council can be said to have influenced Philip in his policy making, the Council of State and later the Council of War were by far the most important, simply because foreign policy occupied so much of his working day and he was at war for all but seven years of his reign (**167**). At first the composition of the Council of State reflected Charles's cosmopolitan outlook. However, on his return to Spain in 1559 Philip altered its complexion, which set the tone for the next twenty years: Cardinal Granvelle remained in the Netherlands, the Duke of Savoy and Andrea Doria of Genoa went home to Italy, and apart from Gonzalo Pérez, the King's personal secretary between 1543 and 1566, only Ruy Gómez de Silva (the Prince of Eboli), the Duke of Alva, Juan Manrique de Lara and Antonio de Toledo remained. The vacancies were quickly filled by the clients and protégés of Eboli and Alva, whose personal rivalry characterised this first administration. Traditionally, historians have claimed that the main difference between these factions was Alva's love of war and Eboli's belief in peaceful diplomacy, but more recently this view has been criticised – firstly by Henry Kamen, who suggests that such distinctions are unwise since neither faction held fixed views on foreign affairs and both regularly shifted their ground according to prevailing winds; and secondly by Dr Lovett, who believes that the key issue dividing them was whether Spain should have a centralist or federal administration (**70, 97, 104**). It is likely that Philip actively encouraged this factionalism, thereby ensuring that neither group became dominant while at the same time he was supplied with a ready source of information. The key figure in this ministry was probably Gonzalo Pérez. As secretary to the council he was able to speak privately with the King and assist in shaping his attitude to matters under discussion; moreover, it was he who relayed the King's responses to the councillors' recommendations. The importance of his office was revealed at his death, when Eboli and Alva pressed Philip to appoint their respective clients, Antonio Pérez and Gabriel de Zayas. Typically, Philip compromised and divided the post between them. The deep rivalry, not unlike that of Leicester and Burghley at the English court, survived the death of Eboli in 1573 because Pérez had eclipsed Alva as Philip's principal adviser following the general's failure in the Netherlands. In 1579, however, this 'first' ministry suddenly came to an end with the disgrace of both Alva and Pérez.

In the early 1570s Philip suspected that his half-brother, Don John, wanted to establish a kingdom for himself, possibly in North Africa or England, and so needed careful watching. Pérez suggested that an informant at the prince's court was needed, and for three years one of his protégés, Juan de Escobedo, fulfilled this role, but Philip never liked him and found his incessant demands for rewards increasingly tiresome. Escobedo believed Pérez had altered correspondence between Don John and Philip to make it look as if Don John was behaving treasonably and to ensure that his ideas concerning the Netherlands were not adopted. When Escobedo unexpectedly arrived in Madrid in 1578 to find out what had been going on, he began to get his own back by spreading rumours that Pérez was having an affair with the singularly attractive one-eyed Princess of Eboli, that he received payments from Genoese bankers, and was selling state secrets. Both Philip and Pérez agreed that Escobedo had to be silenced, and on 31 March 1578 he was murdered in a street in Madrid. Significantly, no enquiry took place for several months, and the assassins were never found, but Pérez himself now became a security risk (see p. 22). In the spring of 1579, Vázquez showed Philip the personal papers of the recently deceased

Don John which clearly proved that Pérez had withheld certain letters. His arrest followed on 28 July when he refused to accept a new post in far-away Venice (**109**). While this intrigue was unfolding, Philip decided to remove Alva from the council. He discovered that the general's son had married without royal assent and used this minor imperfection to banish Alva to his estates.

The very day Pérez was arrested, the sixty-two-year-old Cardinal Granvelle arrived from Rome to head the council. How far he was a stop-gap is a debatable point. Seven of Philip's most trusted advisers had died between 1575 and 1578, and with Alva and Pérez in disgrace and the King preparing to leave for Portugal, Granvelle's presence introduced a much-needed steadying influence. He and his assistant, Don Juan de Idiáquez, complemented each other's abilities very well, even if they were resented by the Castilian councillors. The King's return in April 1583 and the arrival of Juan de Zúñiga y Requeséns ended Granvelle's Indian summer. Zúñiga's beliefs differed from Granvelle's in matters of emphasis, not policy. Both recognised the importance of bringing the Dutch Revolt to a speedy conclusion and agreed that England must be stopped from interfering, but whereas Granvelle saw the Netherlands as his main priority, Zúñiga struck a chord with the Castilians in seeing the defence of the peninsula as equally important. Granvelle remained on the council until his death in 1586, but by then he had been eclipsed by Zúñiga, Idiáquez and Don Cristóbal de Moura, who had come to Philip's attention in Portugal. It is probable that Philip would have allowed these men and their aristocratic counterparts to continue to function through the Council of State, but in October 1585 he and Vázquez were taken ill, and, upon recovering, a major reform was introduced. Instead of convening a full complement of councillors of state, the most important business came to be conducted in secret by a select group of three or four close advisers in the company of the King's personal secretary. This *Junta de Noche*, so called because it met each evening before dinner, comprised Zúñiga (until his death in 1586), Idiáquez, Moura, occasionally the Count of Chinchón, and always Vázquez. Most historians regard this informal advisory *junta* as the work of Vázquez, who saw the merits of a small and experienced committee which could pass its recommendations directly to the King, although it has also been suggested that *juntas* may have been formed because their members had little confidence in the other, more aristocratic councillors of state (**97, 123, 136**).

The Council of State never recovered its former authority even though, like other central councils, it continued to function. By 1593 the *Junta de Noche* had developed clear areas of responsibility: Moura oversaw financial affairs and Portugal; Idiáquez directed foreign, military and naval affairs; Chinchón became an expert on Aragon and Italy, and Vázquez acted as general co-ordinator. Philip depended heavily upon these intimate advisers, but their narrow range of vision and lack of field expertise were weaknesses which he had come to recognise by 1591. He therefore made increasing use of the *Junta Grande*, comprising eight to ten of his most experienced councillors, to review memoranda before sending their recommendations to the *Junta de Noche* for evaluation. However, his distrust of this clique caused him to turn to the *Junta de Gobierno* (Governing Committee) comprising Idiáquez, Moura, Chinchón, Archduke Albert and the relatively inexperienced heir to the throne, Prince Philip. It was Moura and not the King's new personal secretary Idiáquez who reported the recommendations of the *Junta de Noche* to the King. However, Philip, who was teaching his son the art of government, had no wish to compromise him with an omnipotent *junta* dominated by either the Idiáquez family or Moura. In 1595, therefore, when Albert left Madrid to become captain-general of the army of Flanders, effective responsibility for government passed to the Prince, who had to make do with the advice of elderly, insular ministers. Not until his father died did Philip III jettison this 'second' ministry and turn to his viceroy in Valencia, the Duke of Lerma.

Castilian administration

The administration of each of Philip's dominions largely depended upon viceroys, governors and royal servants, most of whom he never met and whose authority varied enormously. Their activities were watched over by permanent institutions such as the *audiencias* and occasionally by royal informers and secret agents. The system was one of checks and balances: the viceroy was monitored by the *audiencia*, the *audiencia* by the viceroy, and both were scrutinised by the council in Madrid, which was answerable to the King.

Only in Castile was any real attempt made to centralise the administration, and even here effective control of the towns and countryside fell to the grandees and nobility. They defended the country and supplied the local militia, while the crown exempted them from direct taxation and accorded them their desired social and political pre-eminence in their *país**. As they already controlled thousands of men, had the capital to raise, pay and supply an army quickly and had a vested interest in maintaining law and order, captains-general such as the Marquis of Mondéjar in Granada and the Duke of Medina Sidonia in Andalucía possessed immense power. The crown's principal servant in local government was the *corregidor** (**49**). Trained in the law and appointed by the councils in Madrid, some sixty-six *corregidores* presided over town councils and exercised considerable political, administrative and judicial authority [**doc. 3**]. Although in theory the office was held for one year with the possibility of extension to two, in the later years of Philip's reign, periods of three, four and five years were not uncommon. Their main political function was to manage their local council and influence the appointment of the *procuradores** (local representatives) to the *Cortes** to ensure that they were willing servants of the crown rather than tools of their constituents. This was never an easy task, as became evident in 1566. Philip instructed all *corregidores* to secure the return of deputies who were ready to grant the *servicio** unconditionally [**doc. 4**]. Most of the local councils strongly resisted this infringement of their customary rights and there was little the *corregidores* could do to stop them. The *corregidores* also exercised full jurisdiction in criminal and civil matters, although appeals against their judgement could be taken to a regional court and, if necessary, before the King's Council. Administratively, the *corregidor* and his assistant, the *teniente*, or his appointee to nearby towns, the *alcalde mayor**, were responsible for the enforcement of all royal laws. Once a year the *corregidores* conducted a *visita* of the district of the city to determine the effectiveness of justice and government, and to put right any misdemeanours. Analogous to the Elizabethan JPs, their duties ranged from maintaining public works and buildings to inspecting weights and measures, inns, brothels, jails and markets; from assessing and collecting taxation to securing sufficient supplies of food for the towns. In times of war the *corregidor* had to marshal citizens, provision towns and, in association with the principal local grandee, organise their defence. In Murcia, Lorca and Cartagena, for example, the *corregidor* and town council mustered and armed the troops which the Marquis of Los Vélez commanded in the field (**21**).

War was a severe test of Philip's administration, and in the 1580s the *corregidores* were struggling to keep control. Low salaries for all senior administrative army officers meant that venality, peculation and absenteeism were rife. The paymaster of the fortification works in Cadiz, for example, earned 35 *ducats* a year, which was no more than a soldier's wage, and like other crown servants he deputed his work in order that he could acquire a supplementary source of income. Increasingly, *corregidores* were expected to coerce town councils into providing more money, men and materials for the war effort, but they too proved reluctant to co-operate and many blatantly ignored royal directives. In 1588 Valladolid would not draw up a muster list; in 1590 Seville ignored requests to raise troops; and in Murcia unpopular crown nominees were rejected in favour of traditional captains. The crown was powerless to act, and at times it appears that even the *corregidores* colluded with the local nobles to exercise as much independence as was mutually convenient. The main municipal office of magistrate, the *regidor**, exemplified the problem. As early as 1558 it had been available to anyone who could pay the going rate of 10,000 *ducats*, and although the official salary was just a few *ducats*, constant warfare presented the opportunity of making considerable sums of money through bribes, fees, gifts and personal contracts. Loyalty to the crown existed but it was not so compelling as the opportunities of self-advancement, and all royal servants knew that official enquiries could easily be hoodwinked.

The Castilian *Cortes**

Each of Philip's dominions had its own representative assembly: the *Cortes* in Spain, parliaments in Italy, and States-General in the Netherlands. Each was determined to resist any encroachment on its traditional rights and privileges and presented real obstacles to a government intent on centralisation. Philip exercised most control over the Castilian *Cortes*. By 1556 just eighteen towns, mainly in Old Castile, were represented by the thirty-six *procuradores** who were chosen by lot. It was once believed that the *Cortes* had been steadily declining since the fourteenth century but this view has recently been challenged by Charles Jago (**36**, **62**). He has argued that until Philip's reign the crown experienced little trouble; no parliamentary grant was withheld or reduced in size, and in 1560 the *Cortes* even consented to an increase in the price of the *alcabala**. Thereafter, in response to a series of irritating new customs and excise duties and taxes on the production and sale of salt, it began to insist on redress before supply. Philip anticipated trouble in 1566 and ordered his *corregidores* to make sure that future *procuradores* were not under oath to their local council which would have restricted their power to grant him a *servicio** [**doc. 4**]. Some cities, like Burgos, co-operated immediately and gave their *procuradores* full authority to act as they saw fit, but the majority of municipalities wanted important matters referred back to them before a vote was taken. This *Cortes* was one of the most fractious Philip had to face. From the outset it attempted to get the recent taxes repealed and extract an assurance that no new tax or duty would be introduced without its consent, and it held out for these demands by threatening to withhold the ordinary *servicio* and then the extraordinary *servicio*. A matter of principle was at stake. Philip never yielded to this political blackmail, but he did offer a number of vague guarantees of future consultation if both *servicios* were voted. After much pressure the *Cortes* backed down and approved the grant, but when it subsequently drafted its grievances and requests in 1567, Philip either rejected them or replied evasively [**doc. 5**].

While some historians like Pierson and Griffiths believe that the King 'won a major battle in making the *Cortes* of Castile the subservient tool of monarchical government', others, like Charles Jago, see this episode as an important precedent in which the principle of 'withholding the *servicios* had been established' (**54**, p. 36; **63**, p. 107; **136**). He cites the subsequent objections of the 1571 and 1573 *Cortes* and the refusal of the cities and towns to collect a triple *encabezamiento general** in 1575–76. Their instructions to their proctors at the 1576 *Cortes* to seek redress by withholding the normal parliamentary supply was a defiant gesture which Philip could not ignore. Several cities drew up petitions for their deputies to submit to the King. Burgos requested exemption from the *servicios* and the withdrawal of price controls on grain, and complained about the sale of municipal offices and *señoríos*. The aldermen of Murcia claimed that if they approved the *servicio* they would be 'stoned by the people'. In August Philip offered a compromise. If the proctors granted an ordinary *servicio* then he would listen to the complaints about the *encabezamiento* before asking them to approve the extraordinary *servicio*. The *Cortes* accepted, and on 11 October voted the subsidy. The ensuing discussions lasted several months and led to Philip reducing the *encabezamiento* from 2.5 to 1.5 million *ducats*, which was a remarkable defeat for the crown. The *procuradores* even pressed for it to be halved again, but Philip had conceded enough. By November 1577 the *Cortes* had approved the second part of the *servicio* and, its work completed, it was dissolved on 13 December 1577 (**63**).

Philip's attempts between 1578 and 1588 to impose new taxes and increase existing ones were baulked by the *Cortes* as long as the crown would not concede the principle of redress before supply. Deadlock was only ended when the defeat of the Armada forced him into rebuilding his fleet and the cities were made aware of the vulnerability of their coastline. The subsequent solution represented a compromise for the crown and a victory for the *Cortes*. A new tax, the *millones**, was introduced in 1590, but only after Philip agreed in advance to accept over one hundred conditions. Moreover, each municipality was allowed to raise its share of the subsidy however it liked under the general supervision of the *Cortes*. The principle of prior redress was therefore established, although Philip insisted that the conditions should be discussed only after the overall sum to be granted had been agreed in outline, and this remained the practice until the reign of Charles II. When the *millones* was due for renewal in 1596, the *Cortes* formally declared: 'this service is granted by the Kingdom for as long as the conditions of this contract are observed, and if any of these are broken it shall *ipso facto* cease, and the Kingdom will have no obligation to continue with it'. Thereafter, the relationship between the crown and the *Cortes* was put onto a contractual basis which could not easily be dismissed by either party.

In the course of his reign Philip had faced an increasingly intractable *Cortes*. He had tried to manage them by alternating threats with *douceurs* and, although he retained the upper hand, he had to make concessions. I. A. A. Thompson has suggested that as the crown's financial condition deteriorated, it became more dependent upon parliamentary grants and of necessity convened more sessions. Between 1556 and 1572 five *Cortes* had met for an average of 74 days a year, but this increased to 265 days a year for the seven *Cortes* held between 1572 and 1598. At the same time the *servicio** rose from less than 25 per cent of the royal revenue to nearly 40 per cent (**165**). It seems that the more the *Cortes* met, the more outspoken it became. By the 1590s it was openly criticising Philip's imperial policies: 'Was the war really necessary?' it asked. 'Could Castile continue to afford it?' 'It is not for Castile alone to bear the cost,' said one *procurador** in 1593. In 1597 the *Cortes* showed how far it had changed when it would not agree to the new *millones* to be levied on *sisas**, and by 1598 only ten out of eighteen towns had assented (**63**) (see p. 27).

Navarre, Catalonia, Valencia and Aragon

The situation outside Castile was far worse for a variety of reasons. The *Cortes* of the kingdom of Navarre had thirty-four deputies representing the leading towns and country estates, each intent upon guarding the subjects' liberties in the face of incipient centralism and refusing to listen sympathetically to Philip's fiscal requests. Similarly, the Catalonian *Cortes* fiercely defended its *fueros** (traditional privileges), and in exchange for subsidies the crown was obliged to make legal and administrative concessions. However, Catalonia remained nominally obedient because effective power rested with the nobles, whose attitude was basically conservative **(37)**. In Valencia the maintenance of law and order was a serious problem as the nobles seemed to be more interested in retaining their feudal power than in national security, which meant that corsair pirates could attack coastal towns with impunity.

Philip recognised that Aragon was the key to the problem. It was nominally responsible for these subordinate kingdoms but resented any attempt by Madrid to interfere in its affairs. The nobles controlled society. They dominated the *Diputación**, a standing committee of eight deputies which met in the absence of a *Cortes*. They kept private armies, and they wielded the power of life and death over their tenantry. The King was only allowed to appoint the viceroy; the office of *Justiciar** was traditionally in the native house of Lanuza, and all other officials were elected by the Aragonese. An unsavoury episode occurred at the outset of Philip's reign when the viceroy, the Duke of Francavila, executed a man accused of complicity with bandits. Riots and disturbances broke out in 1556 in Zaragoza as the people claimed that a Castilian could not order the execution of an Aragonese irrespective of his office or offence. When Francavila fled the kingdom a constitutional *impasse* arose. Only the King could call a *Cortes* to restore order, but Philip had not yet been crowned in Aragon and technically the ailing Charles V was still their monarch. The Castilian Regent, Joanna, dared not intervene for fear of escalating violence, and when leading nobles called an illegal meeting of the *Cortes* in 1559, arguments broke out and the assembly fell apart. Normality only returned when Philip appointed Joanna as superintendent and governor of Aragon and promised to visit the kingdom as soon as possible.

For the next twenty years Philip largely left Aragon alone, but government steadily deteriorated and in the 1580s he decided to intervene. There were increasing reports of disturbances between seigneurial lords and vassals, and justice seemed to have broken down in the county of Ribagorza. At Codo a Christian sheep farmer was murdered by Moriscos* in 1585 and minor acts of vengeance led to a major counter-reprisal in 1588. Codo and the nearby village of Pina were sacked and 300 inhabitants killed by a gang of farmers and bandits. This latest episode of lawlessness, coupled with bandits seizing a silver convoy in Catalonia, sharpened Philip's resolve to act. In 1588 he assumed control of Ribagorza by buying its fief from the Duke of Villahermosa, and followed it up by appointing the Count of Almenara, a Castilian, as the new viceroy. This was guaranteed to ruffle a few Aragonese feathers.

Trouble broke out in 1590. Almenara announced that government troops would soon be arriving to buttress the French border and prevent Huguenots from entering Spain, but Aragonese nobles sensed that their freedom was in jeopardy and began a minor revolt in Zaragoza. Apart from Villahermosa and the Count of Aranda, few supported it, but the unexpected arrival of Antonio Pérez transformed the situation. In April he had escaped from Madrid, where he was awaiting execution, and fled across the border to Aragon where, as a native, he wished to stand trial and clear his name. For twelve months Philip did nothing while Pérez revealed evidence before the *Justiciar** of the King's complicity in Escobedo's murder. By May 1591, however, Philip had had enough and ordered Pérez to be moved to the Inquisition's cells – allegedly because he was a heretic, but more probably so that he could be permanently silenced. To the Aragonese nobles this was an infringement of their liberties, and Gil de Mesa and Villahermosa organised popular demonstrations which predictably got out of hand. Almenara was murdered, the Inquisition's headquarters were burned down, and Pérez was rescued and returned to the supreme court. Philip realised he had to restore law and order quickly if Aragon was not to turn into another Netherlands. Fourteen thousand troops were moved to the Castilian–Aragonese border and the *Justiciar* was ordered to hand Pérez back to the Inquisition by 24 September 1591. That day another riot broke out and in the mêlée Pérez escaped, never to be recaptured. In November the *Diputación** called upon all Aragonese to declare war on Philip, but outside Zaragoza few nobles supported Pérez. Within two weeks the army had suppressed the revolt and in the ensuing reprisals twenty-two rebels were executed, Villahermosa and Aranda were sentenced to life imprisonment, and the Inquisition burned more than eighty heretics (**70**).

The defence of royal authority had justified sending in a Castilian army, and Philip now had the opportunity to enforce his rule either militarily or constitutionally. He decided upon the latter, calling a *Cortes* at Tarazona and personally attending its final session in 1592. He announced that he had no intention of revoking the Aragonese Charter but instead would introduce some modifications. As a result, the crown could remove the *Justiciar* at will, appoint foreigners, extradite prisoners seeking sanctuary, determine the use of financial grants without the *Cortes'* consent, introduce legislation by a majority vote in all but fiscal matters, and annul the right of individual members to veto a proposal. Arguably Philip showed his prudence and moderation in this settlement: a minimum of force had been used to restore control, and royal power in Aragon was now much more effective.

Naples, Sicily, Milan and Sardinia

Philip regarded his Italian dominions as his front-line defence against the Turks. Their military, naval and financial resources enabled him to rebut the Ottoman challenge and to defend other vulnerable areas of his empire. In 1572, 80 per cent of his Mediterranean fleet was Italian, the principal galleys coming from Genoa, Naples and Sicily, while Milan, which was strategically situated between Naples and the Low Countries, supplied him with mercenaries and money. His policy towards the Italian states was one of cautious control exercised through his viceroys, each of whom upon taking office was reminded of his duty to respect the local laws, customs and privileges.

The main obligation of the viceroy of Naples was to preserve the long coastline from Turkish attacks. He assumed responsibility for six fortresses in Tuscany, known as the 'States of the Presidios', which protected the land route from Naples to Milan, while the native landowners recruited troops, financed garrisons and provided their own defence. Large, populous and with a docile Parliament that approved a *donativo** on average every two years, Naples was potentially the most taxable of Philip's Italian dominions but it was also extremely poor. Food riots and banditry were commonplace, yet nothing surpassed the disturbances of May 1585 when news of a sudden rise in the price of bread was announced. The middle classes joined the peasantry and urban poor, all fuelled by prophecies of messianic deliverance. The viceroy, the Duke of Osuna, panicked, lost control of the city, and only had his authority restored when the native aristocracy sided with the government and Spanish troops arrived. Philip condoned the fierce reprisals which followed. Of 820 who faced trial, 31 were executed, 71 went to the galleys and 300 were exiled, while an estimated 12,000 fled the city in fear. Although there were no more major riots for another sixty years, Spain's relationship with Naples had been seriously damaged (**178**).

Sicily had been under Aragonese rule since 1282 and was much more subservient. Its Parliament, composed of three estates called *bracci**, was summoned every three years to vote a *donativo**, payable by all subjects. On ten occasions Philip called an extraordinary Parliament to raise additional revenue, and despite (or perhaps because of) pleas of poverty the *bracci* responded favourably. Although Parliament was not a political cipher – it initiated most of the legislation, attached extensive conditions to the financial grants, and held many privileges – it functioned in effect by proxy. In 1556 only one out of nine bishops and seventeen out of seventy-two nobles attended, since the upper clergy and magnates were willing to forgo the parliamentary arena as long as the viceroy did not interfere with their control of their estates and vassals. If he did, they were prepared to resist. When Philip tried to reform the Great Court of Sicily which contained many powerful nobles, he was baulked, and his proposal that Spanish jurists should be eligible for legal offices in Sicily was rejected by the Parliament. Faction was rife in Messina, and the success of a viceroy largely depended upon his ability to play off one family against another, bribe the prevalent force and avoid imposing unacceptable policies. 'It was', in Professor Koenigsberger's words, 'not so much a system of government by consent as a system of cut-throat politics functioning within tacitly agreed but strict limits' (**83**, p. 44; **78**).

'In Sicily the Spaniards nibbled, in Naples they ate and in Milan they devoured,' ran a contemporary saying. Milan was the most recent of Spain's Italian possessions and had no general representative assembly, only a Senate of twelve men appointed for life through whom Philip's governor controlled the duchy. As they ratified all edicts and appointments and nine of them were Milanese, it was essential that the governor co-operated with them. More problematical seems to have been Archbishop Borromeo (1564–84) who saw himself as the champion of Milanese independence. According to Luis de Requeséns, Governor-General from 1571 to 1573, he was more dangerous to Philip's rule than 'an army of 100,000 Frenchmen at the gates'. In effect, Milan posed no problems for Philip and remained the most peaceful of his Italian lands. Much the same can be said about Sardinia, but for a different reason. It was a poor, under-populated island which, apart from its value in Mediterranean communications, was of limited significance to Spain. Real power lay with the privileged landowners, who blocked any measures designed to weaken their social and political grip.

However, they readily approved royal requests for taxation in the knowledge that payments would be passed on to their vassals (**111**).

Burgundy and Franche-Comté

The seventeen provinces constituting the Low Countries were the most recent acquisition of the Spanish Habsburgs. Created in 1548 they remained under imperial rule until 1555 when Charles transferred them to Philip as heir to the Spanish throne; in 1558 Franche-Comté was added to complete his Burgundian possessions. It is clear that Philip intended increasing royal control over the Dutch, partly to tap their financial resources effectively but also to eliminate Protestant heresy which his father had seen fit to ignore. Equally evident was the determination of the States-General to resist him. The deputies stuck firmly to their practice of referring back to their provinces before reaching any decision, and it only required the opposition of one province to a proposal to block the consent of the whole assembly. Much distrust existed between the provinces, each of which earnestly guarded its privileges, and between the towns, nobility and clergy within the estates, but Philip could not effectively exploit it and steadily lost control. The more intransigent the Dutch became, the more irresistible was his desire to overcome them. The result was the most serious rebellion ever to confront the Spanish Habsburgs – one that destroyed all hopes of strengthening their control over the Low Countries and of establishing absolutism in Spain (see pp. 61–6).

4 Finances

If it is axiomatic that the political strength of a kingdom is a reflection of its fiscal and economic power, it is one of the paradoxes of the reign of Philip II that he should have presided over the most powerful of empires and the most incompetent of financial administrations. A healthy financial condition was a rarity in early modern Europe, and, although Spain experienced a 'Golden Age' and was richer than any other sixteenth-century state, its wealth was illusory and concealed intrinsic fiscal problems (71).

Sources of revenue

At his accession, Philip received an annual revenue of approximately 3.1 million *ducats*, comprising 1.3 million in ordinary and 1.8 million in extraordinary revenue. Ordinary rents were a more stable and consistent source of income but their potential for expansion was limited.

Table 4.1   The crown's ordinary revenue

Sources of ordinary revenue (in *ducats*; e = estimated	1556	1575	1598	
Alcabala* and tercias*	938,600	3,090,600	2,700,000	
Puertos secos*	56,000	133,700	156,000	
Almojarifazgo major*	101,300	426,600	480,000	
Almojarifazgo de Indias*	66,600	162,600	261,300	(e)
Servicio y montazgo*	42,600	55,400	77,000	
Seda de Granada*	66,600	117,300	101,300	
Salinas*	37,300	285,300 (e)	301,300	
Total	1,309,000	4,271,500	4,076,900	

The principal yield came from a 10 per-cent sales tax, the *alcabala**, which was levied mainly on Castile, whose *Cortes** was least able to resist it. Since 1534 a fixed return had been agreed which enabled cities to pay a lump sum or *encabezamiento** that was usually collected with the crown's *tercias** (tithes). In 1556 it yielded 938,600 *ducats* and increased to over 3 million in 1574. As the actual value of the yield was lower than 10 per cent, the crown attempted to increase it further in 1577, but the *Cortes* resisted and actually cut the annual payment to 2.7 million *ducats*. The remaining customary rents were modest in comparison. Customs duties collected at the frontier posts of Aragon, Navarre and Portugal (known as *puertos secos**) tripled, and those collected in Seville (the *almojarifazgo major**) and from the Indies trade (the *almojarifazgo de Indias**) showed a fourfold increase. Similarly, the traditional taxes on flocks of sheep, Granada silk and salt, which hit the poor rather than the wealthy landowners, increased significantly. The salt tax in particular owed its spectacular rise to the fact that the crown compulsorily sequestrated privately owned mines and regained control of its collection from tax farmers in the 1560s. Ordinary revenue had therefore increased threefold between 1556 and 1598, but because two-thirds came from the *alcabala** and *tercias* the overall level of ordinary revenue fell in the second half of the reign. Philip recognised that he could not afford to push the Castilian taxpayers too hard (**170**).

Extraordinary revenue was by definition irregular and unpredictable but in general gave a much higher yield. Significantly, the only direct tax, the *servicio**, which comprised an ordinary subsidy of 800,000 *ducats* payable over three years and an extraordinary subsidy of 400,000 payable at once, was neither regularly requested by the crown nor automatically approved by the *Cortes*. In 1558, 1567, 1573, 1576, 1586 and 1592 the Castilian *Cortes* proved uncooperative although on six other occasions it voted both *servicios* without opposition. Because the other *Cortes* proved less tractable and the clergy and nobility were exempt, it was the middle and lower classes in the principal towns who generally bore the burden of the land tax. For example, in 1571 the four largest Castilian towns of Seville, Trujillo, Salamanca and Burgos, contributed 30 per cent of the total *servicio*. In 1590 the Castilian *Cortes* begrudgingly consented to a new indirect tax, the *millones**, on meat, wine, oil and vinegar. Although it was a once-only tax designed to raise 8 million *ducats* spread over six years, it remained very unpopular because it affected basic foods, and there were more complaints in 1596 when a *sisa** tax was introduced on other foodstuffs to raise 9.3 million *ducats* over six years (see pp. 18–20).

Philip expected his other dominions to increase their imperial contributions but he met with little success: the Aragonese kingdoms voted five *servicios* throughout his reign and the Neapolitan and

Sardinian parliaments continued to offer small subsidies in keeping with their weak economies. By 1589 he was so desperate that even Sicily, arguably the poorest of his Italian lands, was prevailed upon for the first time to help finance areas other than its own domain. The King claimed with some justification: 'All are in my charge, and since in the defence of one all are preserved it is just that I should call on all' (**83**, p. 83). From the outset Philip had more than called upon the Low Countries to underwrite his Empire. During his visit to Brussels in 1557 he had been singularly impressed by their wealth. Writing to Emmanuel Philibert, he claimed, 'there is nobody in Spain who has got the money to buy these cities, for the whole kingdom is so poor, much poorer than the Netherlands' (**84**, p. 113). Accordingly, he welcomed the Dutch 'aide' of 3,600,000 *ducats* in 1557, even if it was spread over nine years, and a subsequent contribution of 750,000 *ducats* in 1566–67. Upon the outbreak of trouble, he dictated that there should be collected a 'fixed, certain and permanent revenue from those provinces for their maintenance and defence' and attempted to impose a series of graduated levels of taxation (**125**, p. 114). The Hundredth Penny tax of 1569 was reluctantly accepted by the Dutch States-General because it was a temporary duty, but the proposed Tenth and Twentieth Pennies which were to be permanent sales taxes were flatly rejected. Significantly, revenue fell dramatically from 4.4 million *ducats* in 1570–71 to under 900,000 *ducats* in 1572–73, while the costs of combating the revolt exceeded 3.5 million (**125**). By forcing the Low Countries to pay taxation at an unprecedented level Philip had cooked his own goose; after 1572 they ceased to be a financial asset and instead became his major source of expenditure (see p. 32).

The Spanish laity may have been sorely strained by taxable demands but in many respects the clergy suffered even more. Officially exempt from direct taxation, the Church was expected to pay regular impositions as well as extraordinary grants. The principal tax came from Church tithes first granted to the crown in the thirteenth century, which provided an income in excess of 1 million *ducats* in the 1590s. A similar levy on episcopal incomes, the *pensiones**, was regularly collected by Philip, returning about 270,000 *ducats* a year, and he was not averse to drawing revenue from vacant sees – as he demonstrated at Toledo during Archbishop Carranza's long imprisonment. The three Military Orders of Castile, the *Maestrazgos**, enjoyed ecclesiastical status and supplied the crown with an annual 240,000 *ducats* in 1556. As the administration of their lands had already been granted to the Fuggers, potential exploitation was limited, but in 1558 Philip did absorb the property of the Aragonese Order of Montesa which brought in an additional 130,000 *ducats* a year (**186**). Three further clerical impositions were regularly collected: the *cruzada** was a papal bull periodically sold by the Church to help finance the Turkish crusades, and under Philip its annual yield doubled to over 200,000 *ducats* by the 1590s. The Papacy also allowed a *subsidio**, an occasional clerical tax on lands, rents and emoluments, but at his accession the hispanophobic Paul IV suspended permission to collect both the *cruzada* and the *subsidio*, and not until 1561 was the situation normalised by a new pontiff, Pius V. Thereafter the *subsidio* became a regular levy – Philip received five in all – with its value fixed in 1562 at 420,000 *ducats*. The final tax, the *excusado**, which was introduced with the Pope's approval in 1567, was a levy on the most valuable piece of Church property in every Castilian parish and provided an annual 270,000 *ducats*. Together with the *subsidio* and *cruzada*, these 'Three Graces' yielded over 1.4 million *ducats* a year in the 1590s, a fourfold increase in the course of the reign. Henry Kamen has calculated that the Church was providing through these and other grants over 20 per cent of Spain's revenue, which illustrates not only Philip's control over ecclesiastical income but 'the extent to which a nominally tax-exempt institution was underwriting state finance' (**70**, p. 165). Furthermore, by the mid-1570s neither the *cruzada*, which had been designated to maintain some of the frontier posts and African garrisons, nor the *subsidio*, which was assigned to pay for the galleys, was being used for these purposes. Both clerical contributions had been diverted to cover advances from bankers and to meet other more pressing expenses (**164**).

Apart from the 'extraordinary' income from lay and clerical taxes, Philip resorted to a variety of money-raising schemes. The diversity and frequency of these measures reveal the government's increasing desperation as it limped from crisis to crisis. The selling of public offices had begun in 1545, and Philip, like Charles, encouraged it according to his needs. It usually raised less than 50,000 *ducats* a year, but occasionally, as in 1567, it was exploited remorselessly and some 269,000 *ducats* were received. In most cases, the sales were at a local level, where *regidores** and *juradurías** were keenly competed for by wealthy families. Patents confirming noble status (*hidalguía**) could also be purchased from the crown. Sales peaked in 1567, yielding 74,600 *ducats*, but as fewer than seventy grants were made in the course of Philip's reign, it seems that the aspirant nobility found other, more attractive ways of becoming a *hidalgo*. Sales of *baldíos** proved much more popular. These communal waste lands lying mainly in the south of Castile were at the disposal of the crown but had barely been touched by Charles: Philip began selling as soon as he ascended the throne. Treasury receipts reveal that, although sales were initially modest, they multiplied as Spain prepared for the Armada and yielded an astonishing 357,000 *ducats* in 1587 (**173**). By the end of the reign, about 4.8 million *ducats* had been received not just from *baldíos* but also from the lucrative sale of Church lands and towns into jurisdictions or *señoríos**. This practice was an attractive proposition to rich grandees like the Duke of Alcalá, who in 1559 bought 1,500 vassals in Seville for 150,000 *ducats*, and the wealthy merchant Juan Antonio Corzo of Corsica, who bought the town of Cantillana for 150,000 *ducats* in 1575 (**120**). In addition to these irregular payments the King also asked his clerical and noble subjects for forced loans and interest-free gifts known as *donativos**. As these requests were exceptional, the crown did not expect anyone to hesitate or refuse, but most donors would have been out of pocket as a consequence – the Duke of Infantado, for example, handed over 88,000 *ducats* between 1589 and 1591.

Although historians are divided over the effects of the imports of American silver and the Indies trade on Spain and Europe, all are agreed that without it Philip would not have been able to launch his sea and land enterprises or wage continual war. The crown was entitled to a *quinto* or fifth of all precious metal and stones; to any seized contraband – which could be particularly large (400,000 *ducats* was taken in 1566); and to profits from the American *cruzada**, customs duties and *alcabala**. According to the most recent estimate, these sources contributed 372,350 *ducats* in 1556, quadrupled in the 1560s and, despite several lean years in the 1570s, averaged nearly 3 million *ducats* a year in the 1590s (**95**, p. 253). What was so vital about this heavenly source – and Philip believed that God spoke Spanish – was the regularity of its supply and occasional spectacular surprises: in 1587 it totalled 4.4 million and in 1595 an amazing 5.7 million *ducats*. Lorenzo Sanz has calculated that between 1555 and 1600 the crown received over 63 million *ducats* in gold and silver alone, and of course it was the strength of this collateral that enabled Philip to spend lavishly and borrow recklessly (**95**).

A further expedient resulting from the importation of gold and silver bars was the introduction of seigniorage (a tax) on those merchants who wished to convert bullion into coins; from 1566 the mints at Seville, Toledo and Segovia charged seigniorage at a rate of 25 *maravedís* for each pound of silver coined and 200 *maravedís* for each pound of gold. In 1595 alone the crown received 200,000 *ducats* from this source (**171**). The American mines also acted as a stimulus for finding and developing silver and mercury in the Iberian peninsula itself. When deposits of silver were discovered at Guadacanal near Seville in 1555, the Council of Finance appointed Agustín de Zárate to direct operations. Early reports that its high-grade silver was substantial seemed justified when crown profits exceeded 1.6 million *ducats* by 1563, but its initial success was short-lived and as subsequent profits began to fall so it became uneconomic to keep open. Ten years later it was closed down (**51**). The mercury mines at Almadén proved more rewarding. Although Charles V had leased them to the Fuggers, Philip declared in 1559 that all mercury exports were a royal monopoly and proceeded to negotiate a new deal with them whereby he would buy mercury at 25 *ducats* a *quintal** and then sell it to the silver miners in New Spain at 100 *ducats* a *quintal*. By the 1590s, Almadén was producing 3,000 *quintales* a year (**114**).

Overall, between 1556 and 1577 total income from regular and irregular sources rose by 180 per cent, from 3.1 to 8.7 million *ducats*, but from 1577 to 1598 by only 48 per cent, to 12.9 million *ducats*, according to the Treasury accounts. Rising inflation caused real income to stagnate at about the level reached in 1580, which was precisely the moment when Philip began to embark on his greatest schemes, thereby making retrenchment and careful management of his expenditure all the more essential.

Expenditure

It was a *sine qua non* of sixteenth-century politics that war was the single most expensive item of the state's budgetary requirements. Given Philip's imperial legacy, R. A. Stradling has suggested that 'it was inevitable that such an all-embracing political unity should be in a permanent condition of war' (**159**, p. 30). This view, of course, assumes that from the outset Philip rejected peaceful diplomacy in favour of force. In 1556, however, policy decisions had still to be made, and although it was likely that much of Philip's fiscal, economic and military resources would be devoted to the defence of his Empire, what was uncertain was how far he would consistently pursue his objectives and at what point, if at all, he was willing to compromise.

Ordinary, peacetime expenditure went on running the household, administering ·central and local government, funding the central courts of justice, financing the fleet and army, and servicing the national debt. Philip spent very frugally on his court and household, which was tightly controlled by his *mayor domo**, the Duke of Alva, until his death in 1582. Annual costs varied from year to year because each member of the royal family had his or her own household, but the total expenditure rarely exceeded 450,000 *ducats* a year. Costs peaked in 1567–68 at 510,000 *ducats*, but the deaths of Don Carlos and Queen Elizabeth reduced the total by some 162,000 *ducats* – the Prince alone had some 762 servants in his employment – and thereafter court expenses for the 1,500 permanent members ran to a little over 400,000 *ducats* a year (**170**). Ramón Carande has argued that Philip applied strict economies at the court, but acknowledges that a true evaluation of what the King spent is very hard to achieve because there was no clear distinction between his private and public expenditure (**17**). He did, however, spend lavishly on building palaces and filling them with expensive artefacts. The value of his collections has been put at 7 million *ducats* and the palaces and gardens at over 14 million; the Escorial alone cost an estimated 5.5 million *ducats* to build (**123**).

Administrative costs were comparatively small. As in England and France, the major office-holders were grandees and nobles and were largely self-financing. The Duke of Alva claimed he spent over 500,000 *ducats* in the King's service. Some councillors, justices and royal secretaries were salaried, in order to minimise the incidence of corruption, but the sixty-six Castilian *corregidores** and perhaps 500 senior *letrados** were on low salaries to keep administrative costs down.

Financing the army and navy was the greatest source of royal expenditure, and went hand in hand with maintaining the payments to bankers for the money borrowed to pay for the armed forces in the first place. In the first decade of his reign, Philip kept his costs under reasonable control. War with France ended in 1559 and the next five years were the most peaceful and least costly of his reign: the total expenditure was below 4 million *ducats* a year. Thereafter, his difficulties escalated: the defence of Malta (1565), the onset of trouble in the Netherlands (1566), the Morisco rebellion (1568–70), the campaigns of the Holy League (see p. 78) culminating in Lepanto (1571), and the explosion of the Dutch Revolt (1572) threw Spanish finances into a permanent tail-spin. Military expenses in Spain, Flanders and the Netherlands doubled from 2 million *ducats* in the 1560s to 4 million in the 1570s. In April 1574 Juan de Ovando, Philip's principal financial adviser, calculated that the state debt had risen to 74 million *ducats*, fourteen times the annual revenue, and although this figure may have been exaggerated – Geoffrey Parker puts the total at 60 million – the impending financial crisis was unmistakable. In 1575 the Army of Flanders was costing 700,000 *ducats* a month and the Mediterranean fleet 60,000 *ducats*; by September the Treasury was empty. American bullion, Genoese loans and the annexation of Portugal proved to be Philip's life-line and enabled him after a brief respite to carry on fighting in defence of his *monarquía**. From 1582 he started to finance the Catholic cause in France on a modest scale, but the decade after 1585 saw his contributions rise to over 8 million *ducats*, as well as smaller subsidies to the Duke of Savoy and the Parisian garrison (see p. 76). The French Guises' gain was the Flemish army's loss, for as Philip temporarily transferred his priority to France, so he scaled down his army's budget from 9 to 7 to 2 million *ducats* in 1590, 1591 and 1592. War with England added to the overall state of financial misery: the Armada cost 10 million *ducats* and the damage inflicted by English privateers on Atlantic shipping and coastal fortresses on the Iberian peninsula increased the annual ordinary expenses of war from 1 million to over 3.5 million *ducats* in the 1590s (**164**). Thus, by 1598 it was estimated that some 10 million *ducats* were needed to maintain Spain's armed forces, a fivefold increase upon the 1560s. The inevitable corollary to this unprecedented scale of warfare was an ever-spiralling national debt: in 1598 it stood at 85 million *ducats* and carried interest payments which alone accounted for 40 per cent of the total income.

Solutions

The only way Philip could bridge the gap between revenue and expenditure and still maintain a high profile in his imperial and foreign affairs was to borrow money. Deficit financing was nothing new to European states in the sixteenth century, but the scale of Philip's commitments and the frequency of state bankruptcies were unprecedented. Genoese, Antwerp and Augsburg bankers rarely advanced loans for more than three years or accepted repayments from the yield of a tax for four or more years in the future, and periodically they demanded all current revenues in repayment for past loans without guaranteeing any further credit. Philip was faced with a limited choice of options. Either he could declare a state of bankruptcy, by which he would suspend all financial obligations before introducing a revised structure of debt repayments; or he could create new taxes and try to make the old financial machinery more cost-effective. Both courses of action produced further problems, and in keeping with his procrastinating temperament, Philip oscillated between them without ever getting to grips with the root of the problem.

At his accession the *Cortes** reminded him of the serious damage the foreign financiers were inflicting upon the Castilian economy, and although he needed their loans to wage war on France, when they demurred he seized the initiative. On 1 January 1557 he suspended all repayments and on 10 June decreed that neither capital nor interest was to be repaid to his creditors; instead, the floating debt in *asientos** of some 7 million *ducats* would be converted into redeemable *juros** at a fixed and reduced rate of interest of 5 per cent. For the first time the crown had cracked the whip and it hurt. Shock waves reverberated around the commercial centres of Europe as bankers as far away as Naples and Augsburg felt the squeeze. The Fuggers claimed they suffered irreparable losses, but some financial houses, especially in Genoa, were willing and able to deal with the crown and took their opportunity to eclipse the older banking families. However, Philip needed still more money if he was to conclude his war with France successfully, and before long he was granting *juros* to fund the long-term consolidated debt and *asientos* at much higher interest rates, in order to reduce the short-term floating debt [**doc. 6**]. The fatal connection between the Spanish Habsburgs and the Genoese merchants had been forged.

Between 1557 and 1559, as the situation deteriorated, the Regent was forced to sell titles, offices and crown land, to introduce a forced loan and to seize the Indies fleet in three successive years. Upon his return from the Netherlands Philip tried again to remedy the situation; it was to prove his last real chance. To obtain a large volume of ready cash, he issued a decree in November 1560 which reduced some of his short-term repayments and immediately freed future revenue. He also authorised the selling of titles, jurisdictions and ecclesiastical property and ordered economies in state expenditure. The most promising reform concerned the *Casa de Contratación** in Seville. Since all American bullion was registered there before being transferred to the Treasury in Madrid, he proposed that creditors should receive their payments directly from the *Casa*, thereby eliminating several intermediaries. In this way a central fund would be created in Seville which would act as a state bank and considerably ease many of the crown's fiscal problems. Unfortunately, rationalisation was the last thing that officials at the Treasury and at the *Casa* desired, and they obstructed the proposed changes, although the unexpectedly low volume of Indies silver between 1561 and 1565, not to mention the crown's practice of raiding the funds for its own purposes, probably did more to undermine investors' confidence, and the initiative consequently foundered (**129, 154**).

Philip also appears to have considered reforming the Council of Finance in the 1560s. Since 1556 it had been without a president to co-ordinate the functions of the three departments. As a result, the *Contaduría de Hacienda**, which dealt with the day-to-day running of the Exchequer, and the *Consejo de Hacienda**, which was concerned with raising money and policy recommendations, lacked cohesion and direction, while the *Contaduría Mayor de Cuentas**, which checked the accounts and had the power to prosecute, rarely did so. The appointment of Diego de Espinosa as President in 1568 reflected Philip's desire to reform the financial administration and, according to A. W. Lovett, Espinosa was one of the few men who could have brought order into the running of the Exchequer (**101**). Little changed, however, because even he could not overcome the self-interest and corruption of many leading officials, who continued to offer advice which at times was far from altruistic. Two members of the Council of Finance, the Marquis of Auñon and Fernín Lopez del Campo were both bankers; another councillor, Francisco de Garnica, was a friend of the Medina del Campo banker Simón Ruiz; and Melchior de Herrera, the Treasurer-General in 1568, was a close associate of the Genoese merchants. These councillors advised the crown to grant more *juros** and *asientos**, and from 1566 it foolishly agreed to allow royal creditors not only lands and rents as collateral for their loans but also the right to sell this security on the open market. As the capital received was offset against the value of the loan, the creditor was protected from the worst effects of any future bankruptcy. In its desperation to secure more money, the crown had taken another retrogressive step. When Philip informed Espinosa in 1570 that 'We have no money', the consensus advocated the granting of more *asientos*. Cash would be raised more quickly than by issuing *juros*, and, more significantly, they offered a higher rate of interest to the banker.

The 1570s was a critical decade in the history of Castilian finance. The demise of Espinosa and death of his assistant Velasco in 1572 opened the way for one of Philip's most talented advisers, Juan de Ovando, who became the new President of the Council of Finance at the age of fifty-six. He thoroughly investigated all sources of revenue, the running costs of government, the floating and long-term debts and the reasons for the budget deficit. In 1573 he made his recommendations. First, the *juros** and mortgaging of crown rents must be terminated and existing interest payments lowered from 5 to 3 per cent. Second, the *Cortes* should pay off 35 million *ducats* and agree to an increase of 2.5 million *ducats* for the *encabezamiento** in return for taking control of its administration for thirty years. He calculated that the capital value of the interest would be 80 million *ducats*, which would enable the crown to clear its debts. Like many of Ovando's ideas, the merit of this scheme lay in its intent rather than in its application. Would the Castilian *Cortes* assent to such a high increase in taxation? How would the Genoese and Flemish bankers respond to another suspension of their *juros* and *asiento** payments, especially if they discovered that the crown had no intention of using them in the future? In July 1574 the recently formed *Junta** of the Presidents urged Philip to suspend payments to his creditors and impound the Indies silver bullion immediately upon arrival, but two obstacles stood in his way. In the first place, the *Cortes* made it clear from the outset that it would not agree to the trebling of the *alcabala** and suggested instead that 2 million *ducats* of royal revenue, earmarked for servicing the debt, should be restored on condition that Philip promised not to raise the sales tax for another forty years. Philip refused to haggle, however, and although Ovando won the support of the Sevillian deputy, negotiations between the crown's advisers and the leading *procuradores** proved fruitless. Secondly, Philip needed to be certain that he was doing the right thing, and instead of taking an immediate decision he consulted a wider range of expertise both in and outside Spain. Not only was valuable time and the element of secrecy lost but also conflicting advice poured in. Granvelle wrote from Naples and Requeséns from Brussels, advising Philip to be resolute, whereas the foreign financiers who had heard unpleasant rumours urged him to abandon the initiative. The King, who was totally perplexed, was not helped by Ovando's hectoring admonitions. In March 1575 he reminded Philip: 'We could have reformed the central tribunal of the Exchequer; or we could have dealt with my scheme for raising a large sum to free crown rents, or we could have resorted to "the decree". Any of these measures would have sufficed to remedy the situation' (**100**, p. 18).

For months Philip did nothing and then suddenly, on 1 September 1575, he decided to issue a second decree of bankruptcy. Not even Ovando seems to have known in advance of the announcement. Why did Philip now do this? The Spanish historian F. Ruiz Martín believes the King was trying to free himself from his Genoese creditors and replace them with Spanish and Italian bankers, but this view has recently been rejected on the grounds that Philip and his advisers had neither the time nor the expertise to devise such a strategy (**156**). Moreover, only the Genoese merchants could afford to tie up immense sums of money for long periods of time and each year await the American *flota**. Instead, according to Lovett, the bankruptcy occurred because 'the bankers refused to advance any more money, and the King, in desperation, resumed for his own use the revenues assigned to pay royal debts' (**101**, p. 911). The decision had momentous consequences. The Army of Flanders, unpaid for two years, mutinied in November 1576, sacked Antwerp and so ruined any possibility of Flemish bankers displacing the Genoese. Spanish, Florentine and Lombard merchants tried in vain to help Philip over the new crisis but did not have the capital and international resources to supply sufficiently large loans at competitive rates of interest, nor were they helped by Genoese financiers putting an embargo on bills of exchange and gold. Once more Philip appealed to the *Cortes* to vote both *servicios** before redressing its grievances over the *encabezamiento**. In October 1577, after several months of hard bargaining, it grudgingly agreed, but on condition that the sales tax would be reduced by 1 million *ducats*. However, the King still needed money and, as established bankers like Espinosa and Morga in Seville crashed, he was again forced to negotiate with Spanish-domiciled Genoese bankers such as Niccolò Grimaldi and Lorenzo Spinola (**139**). In December 1577 a compromise known as the '*medio general**' was announced by the Treasurer-General, Francisco Gutiérrez de Cuéllar. Philip agreed to resume payments on existing *juros** and sell more *juros*, jurisdictions and *asientos**, though at lower rates of interest, in return for further loans of 5 million *ducats* payable in Italy in 1578 and 1579. In many ways 1577 marks a turning-point in the financial affairs of Spain. Thereafter, as expenditure expanded faster than revenue, Philip became totally dependent on American bullion, *juros* and *asientos*. In 1580 he candidly told his secretary: 'I have never been able to get this business of loans and interests into my head. I have never managed to understand it' (**123**).

Ovando's death in 1575 saw Vázquez, the royal secretary, gain the King's ear from 1578 to 1591. He pragmatically urged Philip to cut back on his imperial commitments, but as this was rejected out of hand all that Vázquez could do was to ensure that every enterprise was meticulously costed. Special committees drew up detailed plans and financiers were approached in advance. In February 1587, for example, two members of the Armada *junta*, Juan Fernández de

Espinosa and Rodrigo Vázquez, reported that the crown could anticipate 7 million *ducats* for that financial year: they had calculated the yield expected from the Indies *flota** and had negotiated loans from Agustín Spinola, the Fuggers and the Marquis of Auñon. The 1580s and 1590s saw the practice of assigning regular revenues to finance specific aspects of naval and military expenditure, a procedure known as *consignación**. One of the best known *asentistas** was Juan Pascual, a Madrid banker who was appointed paymaster of the Guards of Castile in 1587 in return for an *asiento* worth 13,000 *ducats*, and in the 1590s bought the *asientos* for the Artillery, Spanish galleys and most of the Land Forces, worth a total of over 1 million *ducats* (**164**).

In November 1596 Philip tried once more to break the Genoese stranglehold on his finances when for the third time he issued a decree of bankruptcy and suspended all repayments. Whether he was seeking more competitive rates from the Italians or was genuinely hoping that Portuguese financiers would displace them is not known, but as in 1575 the announcement was entirely unexpected and, as in 1577, the outcome equally predictable. One year later, on 29 December 1597, another '*medio general*'* was announced by which *juros* worth 7 million *ducats* were sold in return for further loans at rates of interest reduced from 60 per cent to 10 per cent. No doubt Philip felt he had struck a good deal, but the real beneficiaries were the four principal creditors, Piccamiglio, Spinola and Grimaldi from Genoa and Francisco de Maluenda from Burgos (**12**). The King simply could not win these trials of strength with the Genoese bankers. His short-term gains carried long-term penalties which, like the 'Emperor's clothes', were fully apparent to those who chose to see but always eluded the Prudent King. Finances were his blind spot. 'I cannot tell a good memorial on the subject from a bad one', he once confessed to Vázquez, 'and I do not wish to break my brains trying to comprehend something which I do not understand now nor have ever understood in all my days' (**123**). It was a sad but true admission.

5 The Economy

Population

A great deal of demographic research has been conducted in recent years, and despite the unreliable nature of the censuses and *relaciones** of Philip's reign, a discernible if fragmentary picture has emerged. Since the fifteenth century Spain's population had been steadily rising and at Philip's accession stood at about 6.5 million. The greatest growth occurred between 1530 and 1570, before peaking in the 1580s and slowly declining thereafter. In the 1590s Spain's population stood at between 7 and 8 million.

The restoration of royal authority by the Catholic Kings had brought internal stability and prosperity to Spain which, when allied to its well-established woollen industry in the north, the recently acquired American trade in the south and various improvements in land cultivation in the east, produced the mid-sixteenth century population explosion. There were, however, pronounced regional variations which boded ill for the future. Most notable was Castile's demographic superiority. In 1530 nearly 75 per cent of the country's population lived there, compared with 15 per cent in Aragon, Catalonia and Valencia; sixty years later, more than 80 per cent of the nation lived in Castile (**155**). Its principal towns saw dramatic increases between 1530 and 1561: Cadiz grew from 3,300 to 6,000, Burgos from 8,600 to 21,700, and Salamanca from 13,400 to 25,200 (**3**). The greatest growth took place in northern Castile. Bilbao, Burgos, Santander, Segovia and León owed their expansion to the flourishing wool trade with Flanders and commercial links with England and France. As long as trade prospered, farmers produced more food to sustain the textile workers whose growing wages encouraged financiers to re-invest their profits in local trades and industry, all of which stimulated a burgeoning society (**45**). This economic prosperity was abruptly halted by the Dutch Revolt which, in the 1580s, embroiled England and France. Although alternative markets to Antwerp and Bruges were found at Nantes and

Rouen, changing fashions and more competitive prices from northern countries reduced the demand for Spanish wool.

Recent studies of the population of central Castilian towns have demonstrated the importance of Philip's decision to move his capital to Madrid in 1561. Valladolid and Toledo and their surrounding villages had been steadily growing, but from 1560 their population levels began to fall. In contrast, by 1591 Madrid's population had more than doubled, but in so doing it drained the nearby towns of their agricultural and commercial wealth without offering any reciprocal economic benefits. As crop yields fell, so infant death-rates rose and communities were ravaged by recurrent plague. Once an area became impoverished, it was more vulnerable to epidemics and subsistence crises which in turn increased the incidence of mortality. Thus, in the 1590s Valladolid and Toledo showed a fall in the number of births, and the once-flourishing town of Puente de Duero was semi-deserted (**6, 150**).

Spain's leading demographic historian, F. Ruiz Martín, has highlighted the steady drift of people away from the north and centre towards the southern provinces, particularly Andalucía. Increasing tax demands and the effects of plague, famine and war caused many peasants and craftsmen to emigrate to the fertile valley of the Guadalquivir, where the thriving towns of Seville, Cadiz, Córdoba and Málaga had been further enriched by their American trade. High levels of employment were sustained by local industries, agriculture, commerce and trade. By 1591 one-fifth of all Castilians lived in Andalucía, although its population was unevenly distributed. At Córdoba, for instance, numbers rose from 28,000 in 1530 to over 50,000 in 1571 before starting to decline; by 1591, its population was 45,000 and falling (**41**).

The eastern kingdoms reached their greatest rate of expansion later than Castile. Aragon and Catalonia had poor economies and lost many men to the exigencies of war and an epidemic of 1589–92, although losses were compensated in part by increasing numbers of emigrants from Languedoc, Gascony and Auvergne who had been attracted by higher wages and comparatively cheaper land prices (**177**). Valencia and Murcia also showed a belated increase in the decade after 1580 and 1586 respectively, but whereas Valencia began to decline in the 1590s, following the Barcelona epidemic of 1586–92, Murcia remained stable well into the seventeenth century (**18, 20**).

Agriculture

For much of the sixteenth century Spain experienced severe agrarian problems. As the population grew and the demand for food increased, farmers realised that arable farming would be more profitable than sheep. In theory this was true, and regular crops were grown in the more fertile areas along narrow coastal plains and river valleys. However, most of Spain was not blessed with good fertile soil. Over one-sixth of the country was above the 1,000-metre level, and the mountain slopes were only suitable for pasture and woodland. Much of the Mediterranean coast was left untilled for fear of pirate attacks, and large areas of central Spain were arid and unproductive. In practice, perhaps as little as one-third of the land was cultivable (**12**).

Andalucía was the most prosperous of Spanish provinces, producing lemons, oranges, olives, grapes, wheat and raw silk (**134**). Most cereals were grown in Old Castile, and in good years grain was exported, but many regions struggled to be self-sufficient and some – like Valencia and the Basque provinces – regularly imported wheat. A series of bad harvests which coincided with a sharp rise in demand in the 1560s and 1570s saw many cities import grain from as far away as the Baltic and the Canaries as well as from their usual suppliers in North Africa and Sicily. Government attempts in 1558 to curb the rising food prices and stem the shortages proved ineffectual. By the 1580s the whole of Spain was importing wheat and making do with bread substitutes.

As arable farmers tried to meet the growing demand from the towns and cities, so the pastoral farmers struggled to come to terms with their declining woollen industry. The saturation of the Antwerp wool market in the 1550s, allied to the sharp rise in grain prices, saw farmers turn from pasture to arable. In 1563 the crown tried to protect the *Mesta**, which supervised the transhumance of flocks along the royal sheep-walks, by exempting it from tax increases, but three years later its fate was sealed when foreign bankers gained the right to export silver coins rather than wool-clip. The subsequent drift to the towns of unemployed peasants served to intensify the existing social and economic problems (**75, 113**).

Trade and commerce

Spain's trade in 1556 was potentially very prosperous. The northwest provinces of Galicia, Asturias and the Basque region imported food from northern Europe in return for Castilian wool and Biscayan iron and fish; the wealthy north Castilian towns owed their prosperity to the wool trade with Flanders and commercial links with western Europe; the Atlantic trade enriched the southern towns and ports; and the Mediterranean coast maintained its traditional trading links with Italy and the Levant. Although most of Spain's trade was seaborne, wool, cloth, silk, wine, fruit and iron were extensively traded both within and beyond the peninsula. In addition there was considerable commercial activity. In the 1570s twenty-two fairs operated in New Castile alone; and in the small town of Tendilla the spring fair attracted merchants from Madrid, Toledo, Cuenca and Segovia as well as Portugal (**12**). The growth in population demanded more manufactures, while the enormous volume of American bullion entering Spain in the second half of the sixteenth century stimulated trade and commerce.

Even at Philip's accession, however, economic storm clouds were gathering. First, Spain was not an economic unit. Each region was autonomous and towns sought to be self-sufficient in most basic needs. A poor inland transport network and endemic local banditry ensured there was little trade between regions except for specialised requirements by the wealthy and urban classes, and when Aragonese merchants traded at Medina del Campo in Castile they found that they were discriminated against 'like foreigners'. Numerous tolls on rivers, roads and bridges further handicapped inland movement of goods; some forty-six tolls impeded the overland routes to Portugal and thirty-nine customs posts operated on the Castilian frontiers with Navarre, Aragon and Valencia. Second, Castile essentially imported finished articles and exported raw materials. She received cloth, naval supplies, metals, cereals and paper from Europe and hides, copper, tobacco, chocolate, sugar, indigo, cochineal, gold and silver from America. In contrast she sent wool, iron, salt, wine, olives, oil, fruit and silk to most areas of Europe, but only grain, biscuits, wine and oil to the Indies, because that was all their emigrants requested (**148**). Meanwhile, Genoese, Flemish, German and Italian merchants used their financial influence in Spain as an entrée for future trading and commercial ventures.

Until the sixteenth century raw wool had been the basis of Castile's commercial prosperity, but in the 1560s the demand from the great Flemish textile towns began to fall. In 1567 Guicciardini, a Florentine merchant working in Bruges, wrote that yearly imports from Spain had fallen from 40,000 sacks of wool to 25,000 sacks and blamed the decline on changing fashions, foreign competition and the disruptive effects of the Dutch Revolt, which made the market nervous (**135**). The decline of the wool trade had important repercussions for central Castilian towns like Burgos and Medina del Campo. In 1494 a *Consulado de Mar** had been established to manage the commercial affairs of Burgalesian merchants, and its leading members formed a 'university' to provide insurance policies for ships and their equipment, merchandise and crews (**3**). At its height of trading activity between 1565 and 1573 more than 8,000 policies were issued, but as war and taxation drained ships, men and merchants' money away from shipping and overseas trade, so Burgos declined. Simón Ruiz's lamentation in 1570 that 'the trade of Burgos is almost completely exhausted' may have been an exaggeration but twenty years later it was certainly true (**70**, p. 227).

Medina del Campo was Spain's most important commercial town. Twice a year it staged an international fair: in the spring, when Spanish retailers bought materials and goods, often on credit; and in the autumn, when debts were paid out of the profits made from the harvests. The volume of trade, and the concomitant deposit banking and credit facilities, attracted around 2,000 merchants and financiers. As there was no state bank the crown borrowed from the same financiers as other merchants, and any delay in its repayments seriously affected their livelihood and created a cash-flow crisis at the fair. The moratorium of 1575, for example, shook the confidence of bankers like Simón Ruiz who thereafter diversified his capital by drawing up bills of exchange in Madrid and Seville to avoid the risk of future postponement in Medina. When Seville set up an Exchange in 1583 to trade throughout the year, Medina introduced a third fair to bring repayment dates nearer to loan contracts. Confidence seems to have been restored until the state bankruptcy decree of 1596 sounded the death-knell of trade fairs in general and Medina del Campo in particular (**88**).

In contrast to the declining woollen and commercial towns in the north, Andalucían Seville became Philip's jewel in the crown. H. and P. Chaunu have examined the records of the *Casa de Contratación**, the House of Trade, which licensed all vessels, goods and passengers travelling between Spain and the Americas, and their study shows that the total tonnage of merchandise leaving Seville increased from an annual average of 3,000 in 1555 to 30,000 in 1585. It then fell in the 1590s as a result of the shortage of ships and increases in the price of freight before reaching a record level of 45,000 in 1608 (**22**). Primarily the crown viewed the colonies as a source of bullion and exotic commodities rather than as a market for Spanish products. Spanish merchants were guaranteed an increasing profit from the Indies silver and so were willing to export foreign products rather than low-valued native goods (**132**). Seville's prosperity was therefore illusory. Very little American bullion entered its money supply and most of its wealth came from foreign trade. From 1566 its commerce suffered further damage, since merchants were now allowed to export specie instead of native commodities. As a result, in 1570–71 over 7 million *ducats* in silver entered and left Seville, and in the 1580s each year at least 1 million *ducats* went to the Far East in Portuguese ships to settle outstanding trade deficits.

It was once argued – most notably by the American historian Earl J. Hamilton – that 'the abundant mines of America were the principal cause of the Price Revolution in Spain' (**56**, p. 301). While modern historians agree that Spain experienced an inflation rate of some 400 per cent in the course of the sixteenth century, Nadal Oller has shown that the annual rate of inflation was 2.8 per cent in 1501–62 but only 1.3 per cent in 1562–1600 when the full impact of the American bullion was at its greatest, which suggests that the volume of goods and level of demand and production were more vital influences (**119**). Pierre Vilar has emphasised the importance of bills of exchange, credit facilities, *juros** and *censos** which inflated the economy, while Henry Kamen has seen the smuggling, hoarding and illegal export of bullion as crucial causes of price inflation (**68**, **176**) [**doc. 7**].

If most historians no longer believe inflation was such a serious challenge to Spanish trade and commerce in Philip II's reign, they are in no doubt that war was. It disrupted internal trade and transport, deterred potential investors from risking their capital in domestic and foreign enterprises, and presented competitors with the opportunity of seizing commercial markets. Mediterranean trade had been declining well before Philip's reign, largely as a result of the wars between Turkey and Persia in the east, and between France and Spain in the Levant, but also on account of pirates and corsairs preying on Spanish ships in the west. The subsequent demand in western Europe for grain, fish, leather, textiles and pepper saw the vacuum in west Mediterranean trade filled by merchants from Poland, Russia, England, France and the Netherlands, who still traded with Spain despite a Spanish embargo of 1586. One beneficial result of the Dutch Revolt and the predatory activity of English privateers was the strengthening of the size and quality of the

Spanish royal navy. Increasing attacks upon the *flota** led to the establishment of two royal fleets. By 1587 Philip had 106 ships in his High Seas Fleet, and by 1598 an *Armada del Mar Océano** of sixty-seven galleys and galleons had been created to protect the Indies fleet. These lighter and faster roundships of between 50 and 300 tons proved very effective at warding off privateers, but they came too late to salvage Spain's commercial supremacy.

Industry

Mid-sixteenth-century Spain had a plentiful supply of raw materials and seemed well capable of sustaining an industrial base. Mercury, silver, copper, lead, iron and alum mines produced valuable raw materials; leather, hides and woollen textiles were well established in Castile; Seville was noted for its pottery, soap and armaments production, Bilbao and Barcelona for shipbuilding, and Valencia and Granada for silk materials. In addition, unlike most agrarian societies whose low income levels and limited demand for industrial products imposed limitations on the size of their market, the Spanish aristocracy, nobility and bourgeoisie had enough wealth to stimulate domestic industries and to capitalise on their American monopoly.

Against these advantages, Spain was beset by serious difficulties. First, town guilds held privileges which discouraged innovation and initiative and resented attempts by the crown to regulate or change traditional trades and industries. In Barcelona there were sixty-four guilds in 1600, whose entrenched self-interest militated against state intervention. Only where industries fell outside the guild system – for instance, soap, glass, paper and printing – or where the state exercised a monopoly, as in shipbuilding and the manufacture of gunpowder and munitions, was there any significant modernisation (**175**). Second, Spain's industrial platform was fundamentally flawed. Exports had expanded and industries flourished for much of the sixteenth century, due in part to the demand from overseas markets for Castilian raw materials and luxury goods like gloves and swords but also to the moratorium imposed by the government on the export of Spanish bullion, which made more money available for investment in domestic trade and industry. Philip's decision in 1566 to allow merchants to export bullion instead of goods led to a drain of potential capital for investment and unfortunately coincided with the outbreak of the Dutch Revolt and subsequent collapse of Antwerp. Third, some of the wealthiest groups showed a lack of business acumen. At a time when they should have been investing in native manufacturing industries and trying to meet the demands of the American market, merchants preferred to import quality goods and to re-export foreign finished items or to invest in *censos** and *juros** rather than risk their capital in industrial projects. This failure on the part of the bourgeoisie to continue the spirit of enterprise shown by their ancestors has been described as 'an act of betrayal' by Fernand Braudel; but other historians suggest that it was not so much a case of missed opportunities as of the inability of financiers to build up enough capital to invest confidently in major enterprises. 'More than anything', writes Pierre Vilar, 'it is lack of time, for the risks are very great due to the greediness of the foreigner and the sovereign and to the irregularity of the *flotas*' (**176**, p. 140). Although it is a myth to suggest that the landowning classes rejected the idea of investing in trade and industry on social grounds, it remains true that government bonds and the public debt offered a more attractive return (**47, 138**) (see p. 34).

Finally, Philip's defensive and offensive foreign policy accentuated Spain's existing industrial problems and created several new ones. In essence the crown never had enough arsenals and munition houses to make, repair and develop its weapons, and most artillery supplies had to be imported. Hungarian copper, English lead and tin, Italian sulphur and gunpowder, German and Dutch cannon and armour, and Portuguese pikes and arquebuses were vital to Spain's war effort. In 1576 Philip tried to overcome these shortages by prohibiting the export of saltpetre, gunpowder and small arms, regulating their price and quality of production and bringing all industries related to munitions under royal control. Yet even though output doubled, there were still grave shortages. In the 1588 Armada, for example, none of the 2,431 pieces of bronze artillery was made from Spanish copper or tin, and most of the gunpowder and every cannonball had been imported. State shipbuilding was further handicapped by the acute shortage of skilled craftsmen and engineers. To encourage investors in Bilbao, Philip introduced state subsidies, interest-free loans and exemptions from the *alcabala** for owners of ships over 200 tons, and encouraged some twenty-five Italian engineers to work in Spain. However, despite these initiatives there were repeated reports of deficiencies in money, materials and expertise (**164**).

As early as 1558 Luiz Ortiz, comptroller of the royal finances, warned Philip of an impending economic decline if the export of raw materials and import of foreign manufactures were not stopped. Forty years later, the *arbitrista**, Martín González de Cellorigo, believed a decline was already under way. 'Henceforward, we can only expect shortages of everything . . . because of the lack of people to work in the fields and in all the manufactures the kingdom needs,' he wrote in 1600 (**52**). While such a prognosis may have been premature because some industries like mining, shipbuilding and luxuries were still thriving, observers generally recognised that Spain was experiencing a deceleration in economic growth which would lead to a recession if it was not redressed (see p. 97).

6 Religion and Religious Affairs

The Spanish Church in 1556

In 1556 the Church in Spain was in urgent need of reform. The spiritual zeal which attended the reign of the Catholic Kings and which did so much to improve the monastic orders had not been sustained in the second quarter of the sixteenth century. Many lower clergy were uneducated and impoverished and the average rectorial stipend of 30 *ducats* a year only served to encourage pluralism and absenteeism. In the diocese of Barcelona in 1549 only six out of sixty-seven parish priests were resident, and at Burgos Cardinal Mendoza only took up residence fourteen years after acquiring his see. In contrast to the poverty experienced by most clerics, a minority was immensely rich, owning castles, estates and vassals, and investing in government and municipal bonds. The highest offices were the preserve of the noble families and provided most bishops with an income of between 15,000 and 30,000 *ducats*; but none surpassed the wealth of the Archbishop of Toledo, the Primate of Spain, whose income exceeded 200,000 *ducats*. The dioceses were also in need of reorganisation: the small province of Álava, for example, had over 400 parishes and there was a confusing overlap of ecclesiastical jurisdictions. Embarrassing disputes regularly arose between the churches, religious and monastic orders, lords, bishops, inquisitors and town authorities. It was clear that the Church's capacity to contribute to the spirit of reform would be more productive if its activities were co-ordinated and areas of spiritual responsibility designated.

Heresy was not a serious problem facing Philip at his accession. The presence of the Inquisition had ensured that most Catholics in Spain never came into contact with heretical movements, but because it was preoccupied in the early sixteenth century with monitoring the activities of converted Jews and Moors – that is the Conversos and Moriscos – and countering the challenge posed by Erasmians and Lutherans, it had largely neglected the spiritual education and development of the laity. As a consequence, many people's faith lay rooted in pagan festivals, local rituals and superstitious practices. In parts of Navarre when there was a drought, the priest led a procession to a nearby river where he immersed the statue of St Peter in the belief that it would bring rain. Coria cathedral in Estremadura was not exceptional in claiming that it held soil from the crib at Bethlehem and Mount Olive, the tablecloth of the Last Supper and John the Baptist's jawbone (**23**).

In the opinion of John Lynch, the crown's control over the Church 'was probably more complete in Spain in the sixteenth century than in any other part of Europe, including Protestant countries with an Erastian system' (**103**, p. 24). Philip enjoyed exclusive patronage over the highest ecclesiastical offices and collected 50 per cent of the total clerical revenue, in addition to receiving money from vacant sees. He had the right to register or reject papal decrees, to deny appeals to Rome from either the Councils of Castile or Aragon or the Spanish Inquisition, to publish or withhold papal bulls in Naples and to act as his own papal legate in Sicily. In effect the Church was a department of state, ruled by the King and administered by his councils and secretariat; lay representatives sat on diocesan synods whose resolutions had to be sanctioned by the Council of State.

Philip's reforms

By far the most important influence upon the reforms of the Church in Spain was the long-awaited conclusion to the Council of Trent (**64**). Spanish bishops had played a prominent part in the first two sessions and Philip took a personal interest in the final session between January 1562 and December 1563. More than one hundred Spanish theologians attended, including the leading Jesuits Laínez and Salmeron, the Dominicans de Soto and Cano, and the Franciscans de Castro and de Vega. From the outset it was clear there were fundamental points of disagreement. Philip wanted doctrinal issues discussed and defined, and believed more power should be given to the bishops over their own clergy; the Papacy felt that priority should be given to clerical abuses and showed no desire to compromise its supremacy over councils and bishops. However, both agreed that no concessions must be made to heterodoxy.

According to Henry Kamen, the Tridentine Decrees 'revolutionised Spanish Catholicism' (**70**, p. 181). Episcopal authority was endorsed and increased, which pleased the King: as a result, six provincial synods met in 1565 and twenty seminaries were set up to educate the clergy. Priests had to preach a weekly sermon, give religious instruction, start Sunday schools, and use the Roman Missal, Breviary and orthodox liturgy in their services. The Confessional became the most important means of instructing the laity to abandon their faith in 'popular religion' and teaching them the doctrine of free will in both thought and action. Priests were ordered to wear distinctive vestments, separate themselves from the penitent at confessions, and absent themselves from wedding parties and communal festivities to minimise their contact with carnal temptations. At the same time they were to exercise a more intrusive role in their parishioners' lives by supervising the whitewashing of churches, censoring paintings, conducting confessions, enforcing sexual propriety and keeping a record of Sunday and Holy Day attendances. For their part, congregations were expected to attend weekly masses, take communion at Easter, and be loyal, obedient and moral. Philip also implemented important administrative changes. He introduced a new archdiocese at Burgos in 1572, seven new dioceses, six of which were in Aragon, and strengthened his control over the 300 monastic houses by severing their links with foreign orders. Inefficient and decayed monasteries were dissolved, some were amalgamated, and a new contemplative Observant order of Discalced Carmelites was inaugurated by Teresa of Ávila in 1562 (**146**).

Undoubtedly, the new spirit of Catholicism was more than a seven-day wonder; the missionary zeal of Jesuits like Pedro de León and the quality of spiritual inspiration which characterised writers like Luis de Granada continued well into the seventeenth century. Philip's reign witnessed the foundation of twelve Franciscan convents in La Mancha, seventeen monasteries in Madrid, and over eighty Discalced houses throughout Spain. The impact of the Catholic Reformation, however, should not be exaggerated, for it varied from province to province according to the personal drive of the bishops, the general quality of their clergy and the condition of the laity. At Barcelona, for example, a seminary was established in 1567, and the 'Forty Hours' Devotion in which members of the congregation prayed before the consecrated Host, was introduced in 1580. Cardinal Quiroga brought about important changes in his diocese of Toledo in spite of the low level of literacy, while in Valencia Archbishop Juan de Ribera began a financial scheme to raise his priests' stipends, helped found a seminary as well as a college for the education of Moriscos*, and for forty-three years devoted himself to the reformation of the Church.

In contrast, inquisitors and missionaries regularly reported widespread spiritual backwardness and indifference. Most cases of sexual misconduct brought before the Inquisition were not, they claimed, attributable to heresy but to 'stupidity and ignorance', and in 1572 one inquisitor claimed that Galicia 'has no priests or lettered persons or impressive churches or people who are used to going to mass and hearing sermons. . . . They are superstitious and the benefices so poor that as a result there are not enough clergy.' Rectorial wages were still inadequate, clerical offices vacant and Moors unconverted. Communities remained closely attached to their local customs, saints, processions, *Caridades**, carnivals and plays, and were determined to defy official orders to ban them. The continuing veneration of profane images in parish churches was the subject of diocesan synods held at Granada in 1573 and Pamplona in 1591, and the Inquisition continued to bemoan the low level of Christian understanding expressed by many Spaniards in the 1590s (**7**). Therefore, the condition of the Spanish Church appears to have been largely unreformed at the end of the century.

Heterodoxy and the Inquisition

In 1566 Philip reminded Pius V that 'rather than suffer the least damage to religion and the service of God, I would lose all my states and a hundred lives, if I had them; for I do not propose nor desire to be the ruler of heretics' (**123**, p. 53). Behind this diplomatic hyperbole lay a basic truism: Philip knew it was his duty as a Christian and as the Most Catholic King to extirpate all brands of heterodoxy from his dominions. Despite their apparent insignificance, mystics and humanists continued to be suspected of deviant beliefs and were harassed by the Inquisition. Luis de León, for example, an Augustinian friar and writer of mystic prose, was arrested in 1572 and imprisoned for five years pending an investigation into his opinions on predestination and grace. The Valencian humanist Fadrique Furió Ceriol had lived in the Netherlands since 1549 but was viewed with alarm by Philip when he learned of his advocating universal religious toleration. Alonso del Canto, a *contador** in the Army of Flanders, was employed by the crown to hunt him down and return him to Spain, which he successfully accomplished (**169**).

Protestantism had never taken root in Charles V's reign, and the discovery of several groups of Protestants in 1557–58 and in 1559–62 in Burgos, Valladolid, Salamanca and Seville brought such frenzied activity from the Inquisition that some historians have suggested it was stage-managed by the Inquisitor-General, Fernando de Valdés, in an attempt to ingratiate himself with the new monarch. The large numbers arrested confirm that the Inquisition was not lacking in keenness, and the testimony of the accused clearly shows that many were active Protestants. Six *autos de fé** took place at Seville and Valladolid between 1559 and 1562 at which 278 people were prosecuted and 77 put to death. On returning to Spain Philip attended the *auto de fé* at Valladolid on 8 October 1559 where an Italian, Carlos de Seso, and four nuns were the star attractions. The King found the experience most exhilarating and went on to preside over four more ceremonies in 1560, 1564, 1582 and 1591 (**69**). By 1562 Protestantism in Spain had been effectively eradicated, but this did not mean that Philip and the Inquisition could rest. Whilst in the Netherlands in 1558 he had been horrified to discover Spanish students at Louvain University studying Protestant works. There followed two decrees: the first in September 1558 forbade the introduction of books into the country and the circulation of literature without a licence, and the second in November 1559 ordered the majority of students and teachers living abroad to return home within four months [**doc. 8**].

The activities of the fifteen tribunals in Spain varied from region to region, but a lot of their time was spent investigating reports of lapsed Moriscos* and Conversos*. In Granada, for example, 88 per cent of the victims condemned between 1563 and 1569 were Moriscos, but following the expulsion of all Moriscos in 1570 the number of cases fell, until by the 1590s they amounted to less than 10 per cent. In contrast, the Valencian and Sevillian Inquisitions went into overdrive in the 1570s and 1580s, following the arrival of thousands of Moriscos (**44**) (see p. 61). The belief in *limpieza de sangre** (purity of blood) saw rigorous enquiries made into the ethnic backgrounds of all groups and led to the social and political ostracisation of Conversos, which further increased when Portuguese Jews and Conversos flooded into Spain. Following the annexation of Portugal, which contained a large number of Jews, a new inquisitor was appointed in 1586 to effect a more vigorous persecution. As a result some 3,200 cases were heard by 50 *autos de fé* between 1580 and 1600, an increase of nearly 50 per cent upon the previous thirty years. In neighbouring Castile, the Inquisition once again found more and more Jews being brought before its tribunals: the 1591 Toledo *auto*, for instance, dealt with twenty-seven cases; that at Granada in 1593 with at least seventy-five; and one at Seville in 1595 with over eighty-nine Jews (**33**, **89**).

Henry Kamen suggests that the Spanish Inquisition's main contribution in Philip's reign was not the persecution of heretics but the reconversion of Spaniards. Regional studies of the tribunals indicate that they were primarily concerned with enforcing moral and Christian standards within the laity: one-third of those arrested by the Toledo Inquisition and over half by the Zaragoza and Valencia tribunals in 1576–90 were ordinary Catholics accused of blasphemy, sacrilege, soliciting, bigamy and sexual activities outside marriage (**69**).

An important aspect of the Inquisition's work was its censorship of heretical works. Unlike other Catholic states, Spain did not recognise the Roman Index of censored writings but instead compiled and enforced its own. The Inquisitor-General Valdés composed the first vernacular Index* in 1559, based on lists which he had edited since 1551 (**14**). Of 670 prohibited works most were foreign books allegedly containing heretical ideas. Among them were fourteen editions of the Bible, sixteen works by Erasmus, and Spanish editions of Boccaccio as well as of a small number of Castilian authors such as Luis de Granada and St Juan de Ávila who wrote on liturgical themes. The Church and the state worked together in imposing religious censorship: the Inquisition decided what should be banned and the Council of Castile, by issuing licences to printers, controlled what should be published. The Index was revised and greatly enlarged in 1583–84 by Gaspar de Quiroga, the third Inquisitor-General, with the aid of the theology faculty of Salamanca University, which proscribed not only heretical works but anything else it disliked. Of the 33,000 prohibited or expurgated titles, most were by foreigners and of a classical nature; for example Abelard, Rabelais, Ockham, Savonarola, Machiavelli and Dante were all censored. Few mathematical or scientific works were proscribed, and although titles on magic were banned, benign astrological works were permitted, contrary to a papal bull of 1585. It has been argued that this censorship greatly contributed to the cultural isolation of Spain from the rest of Europe, as freedom of speech and thought were stifled and writers were forced to conform or suffer the penalties. However, Dr Kamen suggests that although it denied Spaniards access to foreign material, it had little impact on literature and even less on science. The investigation of witchcraft also occupied only a small amount of the Inquisition's time. In the 1590s such cases accounted for less than 5 per cent of its business, which was in marked contrast to the rest of Europe. Overall, Kamen believes there was considerable freedom and that the Inquisition did not inhibit the development of Spanish culture (**69**).

Historians continue to debate the precise role and significance of the Spanish Inquisition (**130**). Some believe that it was primarily an instrument to eradicate heresy and enforce a uniform faith; others, that its main purpose was to strengthen the political arm of the state. Certainly, there was a strong secular element to its administration: the officials were royal councillors, and every state except Naples and Milan had a tribunal which was presided over by the Inquisitor-General and the *Suprema** in Madrid. Each of the twenty-one tribunals kept Philip regularly informed on secular as well as ecclesiastical business, without which he would have found running his *monarquía** so much more difficult. As he explained to Espinosa in 1574: 'I shall always favour and assist the affairs of the Inquisition because I know the reasons and obligations which exist for doing so, and for me more than anyone.' It was, however, neither conceived nor used by Philip as an instrument of royal power. Only on one occasion, in 1591, when he was trying to apprehend and silence Pérez, did he mobilise its machinery for a blatantly political purpose, and significantly this attempt proved unsuccessful (see p. 22).

There is no doubt that if contemporaries accepted its necessity, they never particularly liked the Inquisition. An aura of suspicion and a fear of denunciation surrounded its proceedings: the onus always lay with the accused to prove their innocence, the inquisitors were never identified, and although torture was probably applied in only 10 per cent of the cases, many victims were flogged, sent to the galleys, or imprisoned for long periods of time. Even the 2 per cent who were acquitted never erased the social stigma of having at one time been suspects (**5**). In Castile, where the Inquisition was regarded as an alien institution and an obstacle to racial harmony, the *Cortes** regularly complained about the intrusive conduct of inquisitors, bishops resented its interference into their ecclesiastical domain, and the network of familiars (paid informers) was particularly despised in close rural communities. In Aragon complaints by the *Cortes* of Monzon that tribunals were interfering in criminal and civil cases as well as heretical affairs led to the publication of a Concordia in 1568 regulating the future conduct of the Valencian Inquisition [**doc. 9**].

In all it has been estimated that the Inquisition dealt with about 40,000 cases in Philip's reign, most of them involving ordinary Catholics accused of religious or moral deviation. Fewer than 250 victims were burned at the stake, which confirms the view that this particular punishment was reserved for people who either refused to repent or who had recanted once before. In fact, the Inquisition was an instrument of terror directing a clandestine apparatus of social and political control and a very effective way of enforcing a code of religious instruction and moral ethics upon a largely uneducated and backward society (**140**). Its success varied from tribunal to tribunal: the Galician inquisitors made little impression on the rural and mountainous communities, whereas the Toledo tribunal in the 1590s reported a marked improvement in the people's basic faith and religious knowledge (**32**). Overall, the Inquisition played an important part in increasing the number of orthodox Catholics in Spain and strengthening their Christian education.

Papal relations

In spite of his autonomy over the Spanish Church, Philip realised it was preferable to have the Papacy on his side in order to support and finance his religious campaigns. The Vatican, on the other hand, recognised that it needed Philip to organise, finance and provide the manpower for the crusades against the Protestant heretics and Turkish infidel. Philip's enemies were the enemies of the Church: on that they were agreed. Where clashes occurred between Spain and the Papacy, they reflected three main areas of controversy, each of which was highlighted by the varying personalities of the pontiffs. These areas covered the extent of Philip's control of the Church in his dominions, the activity of the Spanish Jesuits and the conduct of his foreign affairs.

Philip always defended his royal rights over the Spanish Church and periodically showed his independence. In 1559 he refused to let Carranza, Archbishop of Toledo, be tried in Rome on charges of heresy and only gave way in 1566 when Pius V withheld assent to the renewal of the *cruzada**. Before publishing the Tridentine Decrees in July 1564, Philip instructed his lawyers to ensure that they contained nothing that might alter or reduce his authority or the powers of the Spanish Inquisition. Three years later, when Pius V issued an edict banning bull-fights and excommunicated all participants, Philip disregarded it. In 1572 he denied his subjects the right of appeal to Rome, a measure designed to reaffirm royal sovereignty rather than extend it.

A second source of conflict was the Society of Jesus. Philip realised that the Jesuits had an important evangelical role to play in the Catholic revival and he initially endorsed their activities in Spain. In 1558 over 70 per cent of the General Congregation of the Jesuits was Spanish, as were its first three generals, Loyola, Laínez and Borja. However, the appointment of two non-Spaniards, Mercurian (1573–81) and Aquaviva (1581–1615), convinced the King that the

Jesuits were really papal agents. Their arch-rivals, the Dominicans, led by Cardinal Siliceo, shared this view. Siliceo feared their influence, resented their privileges and challenged their metaphysical and theological beliefs. Trouble came to a head during the pontificate of Sixtus V (1585–90). In 1586 the Dominican-controlled Spanish Inquisition denounced Antonio Marceu, the Jesuit principal of the Toledo Tribunal, for not reporting a case of another Jesuit accused of making improper advances to women and for expelling the informer of this offence from the Society. Marceu was arrested, documents were seized by the Inquisition, and Philip called upon the Pope to revise the Society's constitution and so reduce the authority of its Italian general. Sixtus refused, ordered Marceu's release and the return of Jesuit papers, and rejected Philip's request that the Spanish provinces should be visited by a non-Jesuit. When in 1593 Pope Clement VIII actually succeeded in getting a full investigation of the Jesuits' activities, the outcome was most unsatisfactory as far as Philip was concerned. Aquaviva nominated the commissions of enquiry which confirmed his authority; he defeated the proposal that most of his power should be controlled by regular General Congregations; and he expelled those Spanish Jesuits who had proved so troublesome to him on the grounds that they were 'false sons' of Jewish or Moorish descent (**158**).

Philip's relationship with the Papacy was most strained in the domain of foreign affairs. Each side suspected the other of pursuing its own interests, and to a great extent this was true. Although their objectives were essentially the same, they had different priorities. Moreover, the King saw himself as God's representative on earth and not as an agent of the Pope. At times the Papacy and the Spanish crown were openly opposed. The Neapolitan Paul IV was the mainspring of the anti-Spanish concord with Henry II of France, and of negotiations with German Protestant princes in 1556. In the 1560s Pius IV and Pius V clashed with Philip as to whether or not the Dutch rebels should be branded as heretics and Elizabeth I should be excommunicated. Philip advised against the formal deposition of Elizabeth, but his views were abruptly overridden in 1570 when Pius V, without any warning, issued the bull *Regnans in Excelsis*. Relations improved in 1571 as a result of the Spanish triumph at Lepanto, but Philip's unwillingness to follow it up, and the announcement in 1578 of a truce with the Turks, elicited the wrath of Gregory XIII. The Curia's view that the Most Catholic King was seeking to serve his own ends and not those of the Catholic Church was given more currency when Spain annexed Portugal in 1580 and ignored the papal endorsement given to a rival claimant. However, any problems Philip had previously had with the Papacy paled into insignificance after the accession of Sixtus V in 1585. Neither man liked or respected the other, but although this spiced their relationship their conflict was far more than a clash of personalities. Since the outbreak of the French Wars of Religion the Papacy had suspected that Philip was trying to strengthen Habsburg power at France's expense and in so doing was consciously or unwittingly weakening the unity of the Catholic Church. In Sixtus's opinion the country in greatest need of restoration to the Catholic fold was England, and he felt it was Philip's duty to launch an invasion as soon as possible. Philip responded by rebuking Sixtus for failing to condemn Henry of Navarre as a heretic, and for not denouncing his claim to the French throne or excommunicating his supporters. The subsequent failure of the Armada and death of Henry III brought matters to a head in the autumn of 1589, and communications between Philip and Sixtus during the course of the next year were particularly fractious [**doc. 10**]. The King requested that the Pope hand over 1 million *ducats*, which had been agreed in 1587 as his contribution towards the cost of the Armada. Sixtus refused, claiming that the subsidy was payable only in the event of a successful invasion, and then complained about Philip's imperialistic ambitions. Philip, in reply, reminded the Pope that 'there are many reasons why His Holiness should believe me, admit my observations, and listen to my counsel with the attention and deference which his predecessors have shown mine on similar occasions'. As Spanish troops ominously mobilised in Italy, and Sixtus responded by threatening to excommunicate Philip, an open break seemed inevitable. It was only averted by the unexpected death of the Pope in August 1590. The election of two pro-Spanish Popes, Urban VII (1590) and Gregory XIV (1590–91), improved relations, but attempts to secure another hispanophile failed with the election first of Innocent IX (1591–92) and then of Clement VIII (1592–1605), who sided with France and formally recognised Henry of Navarre as its King. Philip's humiliation was complete.

Spanish–papal relations had been at best uneasy and at times hostile. In effect, Philip resented the Curia's persistent hectoring and interference in his affairs, and he felt he was fully entitled to tell the Pope what to do and if necessary to do it for him. For its part, the Papacy believed Philip had confused what was best for the Church with what was best for Spain.

7 Domestic Rebellions

The Revolt of the Moriscos, 1568–70

In 1556 some 400,000 Moriscos* lived in Spain. Although they made up only 6 per cent of the country's total population, they were concentrated in Aragon, Valencia and particularly Granada, where they constituted more than half the people. It was here that a serious uprising began on Christmas Eve 1568 (**34**, **90**).

The causes are not difficult to discern. First, in the 1550s and 1560s Moriscos all over Spain experienced economic difficulties as the government deliberately attacked the silk industry, their principal source of livelihood. Exports were banned, heavy taxes imposed, and in 1561 raw silk from Murcia undercut their trade. As their income fell the Moriscos had further reason to resent a decree of 1560 which prohibited them from employing slaves and initiated a programme that investigated their landholding rights. Between 1559 and 1568 the crown resumed control of over 100,000 hectares from those who failed to provide satisfactory proof of ownership. The collapse of the harvest in 1567 brought them to the brink of revolt.

The second cause was the failure of the Moriscos to be assimilated into Spanish society and the resentment shown by orthodox Catholics towards them. According to a decree of 1526, all *mudéjares** had to abandon their Muslim dress, customs and faith and become practising Christians. Patently this had not happened, due in part to the failure of preachers to enforce conversion and of the state to provide enough schools and teachers to re-educate Morisco children. In addition, there was the determination of many Moriscos to uphold their cultural and religious beliefs, allied with the protection afforded them by Catholic landowning nobles who needed them as tenants. In 1526 the Aragonese Moriscos had also obtained from the crown a forty-year Concordia by which they were freed from the operations of the Inquisition in return for a payment of 40,000 *ducats* and acceptance of baptism. In Granada similar agreements had been made, but the crown had reneged on these in 1559, and in the wake of the Council of Trent there was growing pressure from the Inquisition and the episcopate to enforce the original decrees more effectively. The result was the royal decree published on 1 January 1567 which banned Moorish literature, songs, dances and costumes, and many traditional customs. As the Inquisition set to work in 1567, the Marquis of Mondéjar, Captain-General of Granada and a major employer of Moriscos, tried in vain to safeguard them from a vicious racist campaign.

A third factor was the widespread belief that the Moriscos were fifth-columnists, secretly in contact with the Turks in North Africa and the Barbary corsairs, both of whom openly preyed on Spanish coasts and shipping. The notion that the Moriscos were a security risk was not at all far-fetched. North African Muslims retained links with Moorish communities in Spain and looked for assistance from the Ottoman court and the Barbary states (**57**). Attempts to disarm Moriscos in 1563 had proved difficult to enforce and did nothing to allay popular fears, which were further fuelled by the Church in Spain calling for a crusade to free the country of its spiritual and political cancer. The call was taken up by the Granadan bishops and obeyed by many patriotic Catholics (**66**) [**doc. 11**]. Complaints of theft and murder testified to the growing disorder; even priests were accused of exploitation. In one Morisco village the bishop was begged either to remove the incumbent or to marry him off because 'all our children are born with eyes as blue as his' (**12**). When Mondéjar warned Philip of the impending crisis he was told to hand control to the *audiencia**, Inquisition and militia, which gave Espinosa unfettered power to enforce the edicts. By December 1568 the Moriscos had had enough.

News of the revolt brought Mondéjar back into favour, and within a few weeks he had recaptured 182 villages centred upon the Lecrin valley and the Alpujarras mountains. However, trouble quickly flared up again when it was learned that Espinosa intended deporting all Moriscos from Granada, that the Marquis of los Vélez had engineered Mondéjar's dismissal, and that the new supreme commander was Don John of Austria. He had at his disposal a rag-bag of undisciplined, low-paid, unreliable troops who proceeded to rape, rob and murder their victims. By 1570 the revolt had become a bloody civil war as nearly 30,000 rebels, including volunteers from other parts of the Muslim world, inflicted brutal atrocities on the Christian population. At Manena, for example, the curate was filled with gunpowder and blown up; and at Guecijo, Augustinian monks were thrown into cauldrons of burning oil. Don John more than reciprocated. In February 1570 he ordered the entire population of Galera – some 2,500 men, women and children – to be put to the sword and their town razed. When Philip visited Córdoba in March he realised his policy of outright conquest had failed and at once rescinded the deportation orders. The Moriscos were now to be dispersed throughout Spain and a free pardon granted to everyone who immediately surrendered. This wise strategy broke the back of the rebellion, and its leader, Abenhumeya, submitted. Although his decision was not universally applauded – he was throttled by his own guards in October 1570 – and internal quarrels persisted into 1571, the main areas of unrest died down.

As is often the case in history, the results of the revolt were far more significant than the events which occasioned it. First, it exposed Spain's serious military weaknesses. Don John had had only 20,000 low-quality troops at his disposal, Castile had no effective militia and the coasts had been ill-defended. Inadequate resources were accompanied by blatant corruption which resulted in at least thirty-two captains being cashiered for fraud. The uprising shocked Philip not because it was a threat to his regime but because it was the first serious protest he had faced and he had failed to suppress it quickly. Moreover, it had cost some 60,000 Spanish lives and 3 million *ducats*. Philip's vulnerability was realised by William of Orange, who commented laconically: 'It is an example to us, in that the Moors are able to resist for so long even though they are people of no more substance than a flock of sheep. What, then, might the people of the Low Countries be able to do?' Philip believed the entire episode was a national disgrace which must never be repeated. He ordered eighty-four new forts to be built in Granada and alerted the authorities for signs of future disturbances.

The revolt could have been far worse. The Aragonese and Valencian Moriscos had not risen nor had the Barbary states given much support; but the Turks had captured Tunis in 1570 and there was some evidence that they had considered how they might further exploit Philip's problems elsewhere. Vizierial letters of 1574 addressed to Andalucían Moriscos, German Lutherans and Dutch Huguenots suggest that the Ottoman Sultan was still contemplating a co-ordinated attack on Spain's dominions. For the remainder of Philip's reign, the Inquisition busied itself investigating letters and reports of collusion between the Moriscos, Turks and Henry of Navarre. Finally, the Granadan Moriscos were compulsorily expelled to Castile, Andalucía and Estremadura, with alarming social and economic effects. More than 100,000 emigrants were deported between 1570 and 1573 and some 20,000 died in transit. Philip intended that the Moriscos should be assimilated into their new environment and in 1573 set up a Committee for the Religious Instruction of the Valencian Moriscos to ensure that each diocese appointed twelve Arabic-speaking missionaries to teach the Christian faith. However, lack of enthusiasm and insufficient funds thwarted such plans, and once again Moriscos resorted to paying out 2,500 *ducats* a year in protection money to the Inquisition. Elsewhere racial tension heightened. The arrival of 4,000 Moriscos in Córdoba and 1,000 at Ávila in 1572 necessitated civil protection, and where they did settle they found their farming knowledge less in demand, while professional and commercial skills were generally beyond them. Barred from the Church and the army, hounded by the civil authorities, many became muleteers and pedlars or joined the growing bands of gypsies and bandits (**46**).

Granada itself suffered irretrievably. Fifty thousand Old Christians from northern Spain moved in and occupied the lands and homes of some 259 vacated communities, but one-third of settlements remained empty and the population fell by over a quarter. The Alpujarras region suffered even more: according to censuses of 1561 and 1587 the number of families living there fell from 5,848 to 1,811 (**123**). Some Moriscos seem to have returned to their lands or escaped the deportation order; in the 1570s investigations into their activities made up 66 per cent of the cases brought before the Inquisition. Their growing numbers continued to worry Philip. In 1582 he considered expelling them all, but two years later he opted instead for a further round of deportations. This seems to have stifled the flow of Granadan Moriscos, as is indicated by the fact that cases brought before the Inquisition in the 1590s fell to just 9 per cent, but the problem had not been solved. In 1590 the King again came close to agreeing to their total expulsion. Once again he drew back, and the final decision was deferred until the reign of Philip III (**26**).

The Revolt of the Netherlands

Its origins, 1555–67

Between October 1555 and August 1559, Philip spent all but three months in the Netherlands and was fully aware of several difficulties. The States-General in 1556 refused his request for a 1 per cent tax on real estate and a 2 per cent tax on movables, claiming that they had already contributed over 7 million Flemish pounds towards his wars in North Italy and France. Only after seventeen months' wrangling did they approve a reduced grant, and then only on condition that they supervised its collection and distribution. When Philip recalled them one month later in August 1557 to demand another subsidy, there was uproar. Brabant led the opposition, but other provinces demanded a review of their tax quotas and responded by stalling and vetoing proposals. Only in January 1559 did the assembly vote a 'Nine Years' Aid' of 3,600,000 *ducats*, subject to their controlling its administration. This was an unpleasant experience for the young King.

Philip was convinced that the Dutch nobles needed firmer handling. He was prepared to conciliate them by increasing their authority, but if the King's power was not to be eroded, then a strong Regent was imperative. Emmanuel Philibert, Duke of Savoy, had been his lieutenant-general since 1555, but a more sensitive and reliable Regent was required. He settled upon his half-sister, Margaret of Parma, although she was not his first choice. She possessed little administrative or diplomatic experience and even less intelligence but she had been born in the Netherlands and had no close contact with the nobles. Above all, Philip knew her limitations and detailed her duties before he left for Spain: she would have a garrison of 3,000 troops and a council of very able advisers, but decisions on all significant matters would be taken by Philip himself (**153**).

Religion was not a major issue in 1556, but by 1559 it was beginning to surface again. The *laissez-faire* attitude of Charles V and Mary of Hungary and the unwillingness of many civil authorities to co-operate with the Inquisition encouraged a steady growth in the number of Lutherans, Calvinists and Anabaptists. Such tolerance was anathema to Philip, who began by instructing the Delft inquisitor in 1557 to step up the rate of arrests. When the King expressed his intention in 1559 to re-structure the dioceses and introduce more inquisitors there was an immediate outcry from the States-General. On leaving the Netherlands, he was aware of its unstable condition, promised to treat it favourably and return as soon as possible. That he never came back and proceeded to implement unpalatable policies goes a long way towards explaining why within ten years he was facing the most serious rebellion of his reign.

Philip pursued consistent aims in his rule of the Netherlands. He wanted to establish greater religious conformity, reduce the States-General and the Dutch grandees to political subordination and ensure that his Dutch subjects remained internally peaceful and prosperous so that they would continue to fund his Empire (**145**).

Although he may have wanted to achieve a more centralised government by gaining greater control of the political and ecclesiastical institutions, it is unlikely that he intended establishing an absolutism. He knew all too well that the Netherlanders had experienced immense financial hardship in the 1550s and were in urgent need of peace. Moreover, the end of Habsburg–Valois hostilities in 1559 and growing attacks by the Turks in North Africa shifted Philip's priorities to the Mediterranean; for the next twenty years, no matter what happened in the Netherlands, he would always keep one eye firmly focused on the Turks. If this emphasis was quite intelligible to all Spaniards, the Netherlanders saw it as a dereliction of duty, and historians have subsequently argued that it was a serious political miscalculation (**128**).

Orange, Egmont, Berlaymont, Viglius, Glajon and Perrenot were appointed Margaret's major advisers in 1559. Principal among these councillors was Antoine Perrenot, Bishop of Arras and from 1561 Cardinal Granvelle, who was responsible for keeping the King fully informed. Greedy, haughty and nepotistic, Granvelle sought to accelerate the persecution of heretics, augment the King's authority to the detriment of the States-General, and above all further his own career at the expense of the Dutch grandees. By putting his trust in Granvelle and allowing him in effect to run the government of the Netherlands, Philip committed another serious error of judgement (**84**). Grandees like Lamoral, Count of Egmont, and Philippe de Montmorency, Count Hornes, were outraged by the Cardinal's high-handed behaviour and virtual monopoly of royal patronage. William, Prince of Orange, in particular expected more political power in Philip's absence; after all, had not the ailing Emperor rested on his shoulder at the abdication ceremony in 1555, and as well as being the most recent Knight of the Order of the Golden Fleece was he not also the foremost landowner in the country? William suspected Granvelle of undermining his reputation in Madrid by insinuating that he wanted to gain control of the government (**162**). To an extent this was true, but then Granvelle equally wished to monopolise political patronage.

Philip could ill afford diversionary problems as the crisis in the Mediterranean deepened. Consequently, between 1559 and 1564, he began to make concessions. In 1560 he planned to garrison the 3,000 *tercios** along the southern border of the Netherlands, allegedly to defend it from a possible French attack, but the municipal authorities refused to release any funds to pay the soldiers and tension rose as unpaid Spanish troops clashed with the local militia.

Margaret pleaded with Philip to remove the *tercios*, and in spite of Granvelle's perceptive warning that 'there will be trouble here sooner or later on some other pretext', the King agreed. On 10 January 1561 the troops embarked from Zealand. A more serious concession occurred in 1561, at least as far as Granvelle was concerned, when Orange and Egmont opposed the proposal to appoint more Spanish nobles to the Council of State. Not only did Philip abandon this plan, but he also found it prudent to appoint native nobles as *stadholders**. For instance, Orange received the stadholdership of Holland, Zealand, Utrecht and Franche-Comté.

Perhaps more than any other episode, the hostile reception that greeted Philip's programme of episcopal reforms announced in 1561 demonstrated the strength of the anti-Granvelle faction. In May 1559 Philip and the Pope had agreed to reform the ecclesiastical administration of the Netherlands: fourteen new bishoprics and three archbishoprics controlled by a primate would reduce the influence of foreign bishops and combat heresy more effectively. Each bishop would be university-trained, have two inquisitors as assistants and be financed out of locally annexed abbeys. Such proposals, if outwardly well-intentioned, proved to be extremely provocative: the abbots resented the new abbot-bishops, the grandees suspected that their political power would be diminished and the nobles believed that their younger sons would have this traditional ecclesiastical career-prospect foreclosed since they were unlikely to attain the qualifications prescribed by the Tridentine regulations on Church appointments. Above all, everyone feared that an enlarged Inquisition would result in a Spanish invasion of political and spiritual life. It certainly looks as if Philip intended reducing the power of the abbots and nobles, especially those of Brabant, which was the staunchest defender of Dutch liberties and whose boundaries fell within the new archbishopric of Mechelen. When it was announced that Granvelle would hold this office there was a howl of protest. The Cardinal was later to confide to a friend: 'Would to God the creation of these bishoprics had never been thought of' (**133**, p. 212). But it was too late. In March 1563 Orange, Egmont and Hornes sent an ultimatum to Philip: they would resign from the Council of State if Granvelle was not dismissed. Brabant put further pressure on Margaret by refusing to collect taxes. She characteristically informed Philip and he began to receive reports from his spies in Brussels, Alonso del Canto, Cristóbal de Castellanos and Lorenzo de Villavicencio that Granvelle was acting leniently ˙ towards heretics. The Cardinal's enemies in Madrid, Eraso and

Eboli, fine-tuned these allegations to convince Philip that he must be removed (**87**). As Turkish problems multiplied and the possibility emerged that the French civil war might spill into his dominions, Philip knew that Granvelle must be sacrificed. In January 1564 Philip informed him: 'I deem it best that you should leave the Low Countries for some days and go to Burgundy to see your mother, with the consent of the Duchess of Parma. In this way, both my authority and your reputation will be preserved.' Two months later Granvelle resigned, and in July Philip dropped his entire ecclesiastical reform programme.

In spite (or perhaps because) of these concessions, the King had no intention of letting the Dutch nobility control policy making. From his vantage point in Madrid their desire to restore the traditional style of administration smacked of insubordination and threatened his centralisation plans. Moreover, their links with the Huguenots and factious nobles in France began to worry him – the Hornes and Egmonts were related to the Montmorencies and Montigny's cousin was the Constable of France. As the grandees began to tighten their grip on the Council of State, he came to suspect that Margaret sympathised with them and would have great difficulty refusing their demands for a relaxation of the heresy laws (**77**).

In February 1565 Egmont unexpectedly arrived in Madrid to ask for religious concessions and more political power for the nobles. This greatly embarrassed the King, and he kept Egmont waiting for six weeks before giving him the guarded reply that although he would not stop the punishment of heretics he was prepared to examine the 'methods' of persecution. Upon returning to Brussels, Egmont encouraged the Council of State to modify the heresy laws and was nonplussed when in June further letters arrived from Madrid rebutting his interpretation of the meeting (**87**). Margaret asked for clarification but Philip demurred until he had more reassuring news from the Mediterranean. Repeated 'headaches' stayed his hand until 17 October when, having heard of the relief of Malta, he sent six documents known as the 'Letters from the Segovia Woods', categorically rejecting Egmont's proposals (**42**).

Four hundred lesser nobles, led by Philip of Marnix, Louis of Nassau and Henry de Brederode, immediately responded by drawing up a petition known as the 'Compromise of the Nobility' in which they pledged themselves to resist the Inquisition and disobey Philip's orders. Four months later, on 5 April 1566, 300 armed confederates led by Brederode forced Margaret to rescind the heresy laws and ban inquisitorial activities. The grandees conveniently withdrew to their estates; they would neither condone the nobility's actions nor support the crown in enforcing the heresy edicts (**180**). She was therefore forced to make further concessions and allow the Baron of Montigny and the Marquis of Bergen to visit Madrid to obtain Philip's approval. From his position of weakness the King agreed on 31 July 1566 to abolish the Inquisition and pardon the rebels, but because he signed under duress and his signature was witnessed by a notary, he could later claim that he was not obliged to honour the agreement. While Margaret and the Council of State awaited his reply, which did not arrive until 3 October, popular disturbances broke out in the southern and western provinces. In August and September Margaret permitted limited toleration in an attempt to subdue the religious violence, and with the support of the grandees she slowly restored public order. But her succession of alarmist letters, which spoke of 200,000 in open revolt, convinced Philip that the situation could only be remedied by despatching a large Spanish army. The decision was probably taken after a crucial council debate on 29 October 1566 when Philip accepted that the situation was too volatile for him to visit the Netherlands and that instead Alva should be sent with 72,000 troops (**128**). Arguably he overreacted to a situation which Margaret was beginning to get under control. Indeed, by May 1567, following successes at Tournai, Oosterweel and Valenciennes, the first revolt had been suppressed. However, the King did not know this nor could he have acted differently, claims Helmut Koenigsberger, 'when faced with the double opposition of the high nobility . . . and a revolutionary religious movement with a military organization' (**77**, p. 234).

Alva, Requeséns and Don John, 1567–78
Alva entered Brussels on 22 August 1567 and at once assumed control, even though Margaret remained Regent. She disapproved of his billeting of Spanish troops in loyalist towns and the creation of the Council of Troubles, set up to outflank ineffectual law courts and to prosecute the leading protagonists, and on 8 September, three days after the arrest of Egmont and Hornes, she resigned (**107**). Alva received the titles of Governor-General and Regent. He was the first Regent not to be a Prince of the Blood, a point of protocol not lost on the Netherlanders.

It was Alva's intention to cow 'the men of butter', and the Council of Troubles certainly did this. Between 1567 and 1573, 12,302 people were arrested, at least 9,000 had their goods confiscated and

1,105 were executed in what most contemporaries claimed and many historians have confirmed was a reign of terror (**16, 48, 118**). Among the more celebrated victims were Berghes, Brederode, Egmont and Hornes. Even Montigny, who was still in Spain, did not escape, for he was arrested and in October 1570 strangled in Simancas on the King's orders (see p. 92). William of Orange had fortuitously evaded Alva's clutches, but his estates were seized and his son arrested (**163**).

By endorsing Alva's strong-arm methods of dubious legality Philip had irredeemably alienated his Catholic and aristocratic subjects, the very people who had stood by him in 1566. As further tales of Spanish outrages and news that Alva was beginning to implement the postponed ecclesiastical reforms reached Orange in his exile in Cleves, he organised an invasion in 1568, calling upon the Netherlanders to take up arms not as 'rebels' but as 'liberators'. Not a single town rose in support and in November Orange again found himself in exile, this time in France. His abortive uprising should have heralded the end of Dutch resistance, but the opposite occurred. Orange learned from his mistakes and saw the necessity of acquiring foreign aid, whereas Alva persuaded Philip not to visit the Netherlands. While domestic circumstances may have convinced the King that he should not go that year, he would, as it happened, never again have a better opportunity, and arguably the postponement cost Spain the Netherlands (**53**). In addition, the cost of keeping such a large army in the field had to be faced and Philip made it clear this must fall on the Netherlanders. The States-General's response was to vote a non-permanent levy of 1 per cent and 4 million *florins* spread over two years, but it flatly refused Alva's request for a permanent Twentieth Penny (5 per-cent) tax on the sales of landed property and a Tenth Penny (10 per-cent) tax on all other sales. For two years Alva bided his time, but on 31 July 1571 he declared that he would collect the two new taxes with or without the States-General's consent. Predictably a tax strike ensued and Artois, Flanders, Hainaut and Brabant sent a deputation to protest to the King. Philip was unimpressed and failed to see that Alva had brought the Netherlands to the brink of another revolt.

The seizure of Brill and Flushing by de la Marck and his 'Sea Beggars' in April 1572 caught everyone by surprise and sparked off a wave of spontaneous insurrections in the west and north while Orange took his opportunity to invade from the east. Alva sprang into action, and by December only Holland and Zealand remained in revolt, but Orange was still at large. More seriously, the war had become one of sieges which Spain was unlikely to win (**127, 131**). It took six months to capture Mons in 1572 and Haarlem eight months in 1572–73. Alva had neither enough men nor money at his disposal and, it transpired, the knives in Madrid were being sharpened for his sacrifice. In 1572 Medina Celi, who was no devotee of the Duke, arrived in Brussels to keep Philip informed and reported back that Alva was the principal reason for the revolt. The King decided he must be replaced.

On 30 January 1573 Don Luis de Requeséns was surprised to hear that he was to take Alva's place (**99**). Philip presented his new governor with an impossible task: he expected him to bring about a reconciliation with the rebels through moderation rather than force, but ordered him not to yield to their demands for religious toleration and the restoration of their 'ancient privileges and liberty'. These had first been requested by William in 1573 and would be insisted on at future peace talks at Breda in 1575, at St Geertruidenberg in 1577 and at Cologne in 1579. As long as the Dutch insisted and Spain resisted, there would be stalemate. It appears that between 1573 and 1577 genuine attempts were made by the Spanish court to find a diplomatic solution (**70**). Granvelle urged Philip to pay a state visit, Montano called for a compromise which safeguarded Spain's reputation, Furió believed concessions subject to Dutch guarantees would work, and Requeséns reminded Philip that 'no treasury in the world would be equal to the cost of this war'. Yet the King still believed that any concession would be detrimental to Spain and the Catholic faith, and so the war continued.

The enforced suspension of fiscal payments in September 1575 and the sudden death of Requeséns six months later added to the King's predicament, but in July 1576 he received an unexpected fillip when Zieriksee in Zealand surrendered. This piece of good news stiffened his resolve to fight on, and in September he appointed Don John as his new governor. It is ironic that on 3 November 1576, the very day on which Don John entered Luxembourg bearing royal instructions to implement temporary concessions, Spanish troops mutinied in Brabant and Flanders and totally destroyed the peace initiative. Antwerp got the worst of it: 1,000 houses were looted and 8,000 people died (**124**). This so-called 'Spanish Fury' and the King's refusal to let the states meet to decide how to defend themselves united Catholic and Calvinist nobles who now took the unprecedented step of convening a States-General in Brussels without his permission. All but Holland and Zealand attended and agreed to expel the Spanish troops, establish religious freedom and restore their political privileges, objectives embodied in the Pacification of Ghent in November 1576 (**185**).

Don John accepted the terms of the Pacification when he signed the Perpetual Edict in February 1577, and on 28 April the Spanish troops departed for Italy. Most Dutchmen rejoiced, but William believed the governor was as untrustworthy as the King and suspected that when his fortunes improved he would 'wish to extirpate us and we do not wish to be extirpated'. Orange's refusal to trust or co-operate with Don John caused the latter so much frustration that he soon discarded his conciliatory mantle and requested the troops' recall. In July Philip agreed to renew the military campaign. The Spanish army, now led by Alexander Farnese, Duke of Parma, quickly advanced into Artois and Walloon Flanders, causing the States-General to panic and flee north to Antwerp. Their ability to survive would again be put to the test.

Success and failure, 1578–98

As well as being an outstanding soldier, Parma was a talented diplomat and administrator, who empathised with the Dutch cause in a way which previous generals had not. As the King's nephew, he was ideally placed to succeed Don John when the Governor-General unexpectedly died of plague on 1 October 1578. Parma's task was clear: he must maintain control of the obedient provinces, mainly in the south and east, and win back the remainder, by diplomacy if possible but by force if necessary. Of all the Governors-General since 1559, Parma started in the most auspicious circumstances. Spain's long conflict with the Porte was drawing to a close, Portugal was about to be annexed, and the Indies were yielding increasing levels of silver. In two respects, however, the situation was more challenging. After a decade of duplicity and betrayal, few Netherlanders were prepared to trust the Spaniards, and as long as Orange led the resistance a diplomatic solution seemed as elusive as ever. More significantly, by 1578 the Dutch Revolt had become an international conflict, with German, French and English mercenaries fishing in Spain's troubled waters, a factor which was to determine its eventual result (**183, 184**).

In 1579–80 a mixture of skilful diplomacy and covert bribery began to win over many moderate and anti-Calvinist nobles: Montigny, Lalaing, Aerschot and Rennenberg all went over to the Duke of Parma. He further treated with the six Catholic states in the Union of Arras (1579) by agreeing to withdraw his troops in April 1580, appointing native grandees to the Council of State, leaving town oligarchs and rural elites undisturbed, and restoring the laws, liberties and taxes which had operated in Charles V's reign. It was all that the obedient provinces could have wished. Parma's success encouraged Philip, egged on by Granvelle, to outlaw Orange in March 1580 and press on for victory. The King believed that without Orange's leadership the revolt would probably collapse, and Granvelle suggested that a price should be put on his head (**162**). Orange's reply in December, known as the *Apology*, and the States-General's Act of Abjuration signed on 22 July 1581, which was agreed to by ten provinces, denied Philip his sovereignty and drew up the battle lines for the remainder of the revolt (**93**) [**doc. 12**].

The recourse to violence prompted the Walloon estates at the end of 1581 to ask Parma to recall his troops to defend them and reconquer the northern provinces. By 1582, 60,000 troops had arrived and by selecting specific towns, besieging them and offering peace terms which (unlike Alva) he kept to, he soon re-captured Maastricht, Dunkirk, Ypres, Bruges, Ghent, Ostend, Brussels and Antwerp (**93**). By 1585 only Holland and Zealand remained outside his control, and Orange was no longer their leader: in July 1584 he was the victim of an assassin's bullet. Victory now seemed certain to Philip, who characteristically ordered Parma not to make any religious concessions. 'They are all to embrace the Roman Catholic faith and the exercise of that alone is to be permitted,' he declared (**123**, p. 223).

In August 1585, when Philip least needed it, England concluded the Treaty of Nonsuch and officially entered the fray. His reaction was understandable: war was declared and invasion plans set in motion. Parma was less than pleased, because he could see that Spain's resources would be both diversified and stretched beyond Philip's realisation. However, the King and the *Junta de Noche** ignored his objections, and in 1587 Parma was withdrawn from the Dutch campaigns and told to wait at Dunkirk for the ill-fated Armada. On his return, late in 1588, he encountered stiffer resistance from Maurice of Nassau, suffered his first defeat by failing to take Bergen-op-Zoom, and experienced the first of many mutinies. By 1589 the prevailing view in Madrid was that Spain had to bring the war to an end and that this could only be achieved by diplomacy. Parma urged the King to grant specific Calvinist towns their toleration, but this was rejected. Instead, he was sent back to France in 1590 to assist the Catholic League, and in his absence the States-General recaptured Breda, Zutphen, Deventer and Nijmegen. Ignoring orders to stay in Paris, Parma returned to the Netherlands in 1591, but when Philip heard of this he insisted that Parma should return to France, where he died in 1592 (see p. 76).

For the next two years Spanish affairs were mismanaged by Count Mansfelt, the 75-year-old governor, and Count Fuentes, the acting commander, who shared power and hated each other. In 1594 Philip decided upon a new policy, perhaps upon Idiáquez's recommendation (**136**). The Netherlands would become a separate, semi-independent state, governed jointly by Isabella, Philip's daughter, and Archduke Ernst of Austria, her projected husband. Ernst arrived in Brussels in 1594 but died in February 1595, and Philip thereupon turned to Ernst's brother, the Cardinal Archduke Albert, who became the new Governor-General. A third royal bankruptcy in 1596 left Spanish troops unpaid and further disrupted Philip's plans, and although a financial settlement in December 1597 gave him renewed hope, it was clear that the Army of Flanders was a spent force and that total victory would elude him. In 1598 Philip willed that Isabella should marry Albert, with the Netherlands as her dowry; together they would govern the obedient provinces, while sovereignty rested with the King of Spain. Without having to deal with the rebels, Philip had arranged a settlement which he believed would prove mutually acceptable. He was too proud a monarch to acknowledge that they had beaten him.

The seven northern provinces had in all but name defeated Spain by 1598 primarily because of Philip's commitments elsewhere – his initial preoccupation with the Turks in the Mediterranean and his subsequent decisions to attack England and to intervene in France. Financial difficulties helped to create numerous mutinies in the large Spanish army, and fighting a long war of attrition over 1,000 km from Spain added to the logistical problems. Certainly the Dutch determination to resist Spanish rule and to preserve their religious and civil liberties, allied to their skilful deployment of naval and land tactics, frustrated successive Spanish generals, yet the responsibility for causing the revolt and failing to suppress it lay with the King. He had acted provocatively in his policies and appointments and denied his administrators and generals the financial means and political freedom to achieve an acceptable solution. The Netherlands was a microcosm of his imperial problems, and one which he failed to solve (**153**).

8 Foreign Policy

Aims

The aims and motives behind Philip's foreign policy have long perplexed historians, as they did contemporaries. Leopold von Ranke, writing in 1843, believed Philip 'came to regard the progress of his own power and the progress of religion as identical, and to behold the latter in the former'; R. T. Davies claimed that Philip's ultimate objective was 'the domination of the British Isles and France by means of intervention in their religious struggle'; while Geoffrey Parker suggests that religion was the mainspring of his foreign policy (**30**, p. 136; **123**, **147**, p. 33). In contrast, Peter Pierson argues that Philip was motivated more by personal obligations than by reasons of state, which accounts for his inconsistent policies (**136**). Spain's enemies were convinced that he wished to expand his lands, exterminate heretics and establish a European hegemony. 'The King of Spain, as a temporal sovereign, is anxious above all to safeguard and to increase his dominions,' claimed Pope Sixtus V in 1589 (**104**, p. 273). The papal nuncio in Madrid wrote in a similar vein: 'He says he does not want the property of others, but the chances of the occasion, the penchant for domination which is innate in men, unforeseen incidents, could end in the establishment of a universal monarchy.' The medieval ideal of a peaceful and united Christian Europe had been the declared objective of Charles V's advisers, Alfonso de Valdés and Mercurino de Gattinara, but it remained an elusive dream (**110**, **122**). Most men believed God held a design for the universe, and Spaniards were certain they were appointed by their superior culture, language, faith and wealth to fulfil it. In practice, however, Philip was no visionary and recognised that despite his apparent power, he had insufficient resources to pursue such global ambitions.

Philip's *monarquía* was far-flung and basically indefensible, only held together by the collective will of Genoese merchants, Flemish bankers, Italian and German soldiers, Portuguese and Italian sailors, American miners and Spanish officials (**67**). For most of his reign he could count on the Italian states to support his policies actively; Genoa, Savoy-Piedmont, Parma and Tuscany were reliable allies, while the Spanish possessions of Naples, Sicily and Milan watched over more independently-minded states such as the Vatican, Florence and Venice. The Austrian Habsburgs also gave Philip much of what he wanted: at best their support and at worst neutrality. Ferdinand I (1558–64) was Philip's brother, Maximilian II (1564–76) his son-in-law, and Rudolf II (1576–1612) Maximilian's son. Yet, if family ties were an asset, little love was lost between Philip and Ferdinand, and both Maximilian and Rudolf could, at least in his opinion, have offered him more assistance in his struggle with the Netherlands (**151**).

Philip's prime aim was to defend his dominions and not to give offence. His intention to preserve and secure his lands, people and faith by peaceful diplomacy was noted by Suriano, the Venetian ambassador, when he claimed in 1559 that Philip did not intend 'to wage war so that he can add to his kingdoms but to wage peace so that he can keep the lands he has' (**31, 70**, p. 129). If aggression was required, then it must be a 'just' war; this would not only enhance his reputation but also secure papal support. Philip's enemies, of course, perceived him as an out-and-out aggressor. Historians are inclined to take an intermediate position. They acknowledge that Philip may have regarded attack as the best form of defence, but they also recognise that acts of apparent provocation occurred in the second half of his reign, and they identify his acquisition of Portugal as a turning-point in his foreign policy (**81**).

France

Antonio Pérez once informed Philip: 'The heart of the Spanish Empire is France.' In 1556 and for much of his reign this was most certainly the case. Henry II of France was eager to gain lands in Piedmont and Milan which he regarded as the weak link in the Habsburg chain; Charles V's ailing mental and physical condition since 1553, wedded to Philip's raw inexperience, only served to whet his appetite. The advent of the francophile Pope Paul IV in 1555 strengthened the anti-Spanish alliance, and French victories at Casale, Ivrea and Volpiano convinced Philip that the Italian campaign must be concluded if he was to save Milan. To his surprise, France agreed to a five-year truce at Vaucelles in February 1556; she too was in dire financial straits.

Paul IV, a Neapolitan, was far from pleased. He at once urged

Henry II to join him in an invasion of Naples. Philip decided upon a pre-emptive strike, which was to prove financially expensive and morally provocative, but he knew his credibility was at stake. If Naples fell by default, which Spanish dominion would be next? The viceroy, the Duke of Alva, with an army of 12,000, marched into the Papal States in September 1556 and encamped 40 km from Rome. News that Francis, Duke of Guise, had invaded Milan and was speeding towards Naples brought only false hopes, as his subsequent failure to capture Civitella led to his retreat back to France in August 1557. Philip treated the Papacy with generosity and made no territorial or financial demands in return for his offer of peace. He thereby earned a reputation for clemency which won him the support of all the major states in Italy (**153**).

The Italian campaign of 1557 was in fact a side-show to the main event. To prove he was at least equal to Henry II, Philip first concluded an alliance with England to secure control of the Channel and then launched a major offensive against St Quentin in northern France. On 10 August the Duke of Savoy with 70,000 imperial and Spanish troops crushed the French army, killing 3,000 and capturing 7,000. Philip arrived in time to see the town fall and lead his troops in a triumphal entry. The expected reaction from Henry came in December when 27,000 troops besieged the English town and environs of Calais. The English were taken by surprise and on 7 January 1558 surrendered (**29**). Philip – who by this time was King of England as well as Spain – was furious. Not only had Calais been lost by default; Henry had received a new lease of life, and launched further attacks on towns in the Netherlands. Only in July did Spain retaliate when Count Egmont killed 1,500 and captured 3,000 French troops at Gravelines (**144**).

Already Franco-Spanish peace talks were well under way at Câteau-Cambrésis, since neither Philip nor Henry could afford to carry on fighting. Both kings desired a good and lasting peace but not at any price; although they accepted the need for territorial concessions, they were determined to safeguard their respective reputations. The two key issues – the fate of Savoy and Calais – were resolved when France declared she would concede all claims to Italy on condition that she retained Calais. Finally, a double marriage was concluded between Philip and Elizabeth, Henry's daughter, and between Emmanuel Philibert of Savoy and Margaret, Henry's sister. Philip was delighted with the treaty signed on 3 April 1559. His reputation had been established and Italy would not again be contested by France until 1797.

Philip's policy towards France after 1559 was to keep it politically divided and religiously united in so far as this was possible. From time to time he expressed his concern to Catherine de Medici at the growth of Huguenotism but, with the exception of 1563, 1567 and 1569, when he gave her minor assistance, he wisely stayed out of French affairs (**76**) [**doc. 13**]. Much has been made of a secret meeting at Bayonne in June 1565 when Alva pressed Catherine to act against the French Huguenots and join in an attack upon heretics in the Netherlands and France. Proposals were also made for marriages between Catherine's daughter, Marguerite, and Philip's son, Don Carlos, and between Catherine's son, Charles IX of France, and the Emperor's daughter. In fact these discussions remained inconclusive except in the fertile minds of contemporary Protestants.

Franco-Spanish relations took a turn for the worse in 1568. First, family ties were broken when Philip's French wife died and he turned down her sister, Marguerite, in favour of Anne of Austria. It was a double blow to Catherine, who had hoped her son would marry the Habsburg princess. Charles IX responded by encouraging Cosimo de Medici to cause trouble in the duchy of Lorraine, whose ruler was Philip's cousin, and by openly befriending Coligny, the leader of the Huguenots. Second, Philip suspected that France was starting to probe his weaknesses. In 1570 Huguenots besieged Perpignan in Spanish Navarre and in 1571 he learned that Coligny had persuaded Charles to invade the Netherlands. It was apparently their intention to partition it between France, England and the Empire, but at the last minute Catherine vetoed the scheme and Charles withdrew his support (**160**). Philip was delighted when he heard of the massacre of St Bartholomew in August 1572; Coligny was dead, some 12,000 Huguenots had been slaughtered, and France was again at war with itself.

The defence of Navarre and the Netherlands was pivotal to Philip's thinking after 1572. The rising star in the French galaxy was Henry Bourbon, King of Navarre, who, as well as having a claim to the throne of both France and Spanish Navarre, was also the leader of the Huguenots. Of equal concern to Philip was the behaviour of Francis, Duke of Anjou, brother of Henry III, who ascended the French throne upon Charles's death in 1574. Anjou was a maverick, restless for real power and aware that he was less than welcome at his brother's court. For six years he tried to assist the Dutch rebels until he died of tuberculosis in 1584. His death made Henry of Navarre heir presumptive, but it was now in the mutual interest of Philip, French Catholics and particularly the Guises to prevent him from ever becoming king. In September the Duke of Guise, his two brothers and two nobles formed a Catholic League to keep Henry of Navarre off the French throne, and in December 1584, at Joinville, Philip joined them. 'In truth we have been moved to negotiate this because it seems to be the only way to remedy matters of religion in that kingdom,' Philip wrote to Idiáquez (**123**). He committed troops and 50,000 crowns a month to the League in return for Cambrai and a promise of French neutrality in the event of a war with England, but in practice he had little control over the Guises, who seemed to be more adept at spending his money than advancing his cause. Moreover, the presence of Spanish troops began to cause resentment among Frenchmen of all creeds and persuasions. Matters were going badly wrong for Philip. Henry III skilfully kept Parma's army out of France in 1588 by evading Spanish requests for the Armada to have use of a deep-water Channel port. Then in December, heartened by the news of the Armada's defeat, the French King ordered the assassination of Guise and his brother, the Cardinal of Lorraine. Philip now became the leading protagonist of a debilitated Catholic League, and upon hearing that Henry III had been assassinated in August 1589, thereby opening the way to Henry of Navarre's accession, he was convinced that he must intervene directly. 'The affairs of France are at this moment the principal thing,' he informed Parma (**70**, p. 134). Three million *ducats* were sent to the surviving members of the League, and Parma was ordered to leave Brussels and help defend Paris from Henry of Navarre.

The year 1590 saw Parma invade the French capital, the Duke of Savoy occupy eastern France and Spanish troops land in Brittany. Henry of Navarre's days appeared to be numbered, and when his elderly uncle, the Cardinal of Bourbon, who had a claim to the throne, died on 9 May, this opened up the possibility of Philip's daughter, Isabella, becoming the next monarch. Philip's motives are as hard to discern now as they were then. The French suspected he was seeking to extend his Empire at their expense, and Pope Clement VIII, believing that Philip wished to establish a universal monarchy, rejected his claims to be the protector of French Catholics. In April 1592 Parma successfully relieved Rouen, but eight months later died from wounds sustained in the defence of Amiens. This was a bitter blow to Spanish ambitions, and when Henry of Navarre declared his conversion to the Catholic faith in 1593, Philip's cause became hopeless. Yet he foolishly persisted in challenging Henry IV's right to the throne even after the Catholic nobles, the people of France and the Papacy had been won over. Already the Spanish ambassador in Paris, the Duke of Feria, had informed the Estates-General that Isabella was to be proclaimed Queen of France and would marry Ernst, heir presumptive to the imperial throne, but that if the people preferred a French husband, then Charles, Duke of Guise, would be acceptable to Philip. This piece of Spanish impertinence united the French nation far more effectively than anything Henry IV could have said. In February 1594 he was crowned King and less than a year later he declared war on Spain. The wheel had come full circle. Philip was again fighting France but in circumstances far less propitious than at the beginning of his reign. In 1596 France formed a triple alliance with England and the United Provinces, and in spite of Spanish victories at Calais (April 1596) and Amiens (March 1597), a decree of bankruptcy (November 1596) and the loss of Amiens (September 1597) convinced Philip that an honourable peace must be concluded.

The resulting Treaty of Vervins of May 1598 has been viewed by some historians as a Spanish triumph (**133**). France recovered Calais, Brittany and Languedoc, but she was bankrupt and still surrounded by Habsburg dominions. Geoffrey Parker, however, has argued that the peace treaty 'represented a considerable victory' for France, given her long period of civil war, especially as Spain was by now in a precarious condition (**123**, p. 195). On balance, this seems a more perceptive judgement.

Turkey

Most Spaniards regarded the Mediterranean as the true sphere of royal influence in the mid-sixteenth century. The 1550s saw Tripoli, Peñón de Vélez and Bougie fall to the Turks, leaving Spain in possession of Mers-el-Kebir, Orán, Melilla and la Goletta, a fortress overlooking Tunis (**59**). Philip knew that if the coast of North Africa became Turkish, communications with Naples and Sicily would be seriously threatened, but until 1559 his priority was his war with France. As soon as the Peace of Câteau-Cambrésis was concluded, he was freed from his northern commitments and the likelihood of a future Franco-Turkish alliance. Peace talks with Suleiman I were cancelled and plans went ahead for a Spanish attack on Tripoli. Philip considered that minimum forces would be sufficient if they could surprise the Turks, but his commander, Medina Celi, the Viceroy of Sicily, disagreed. He perceived the campaign in larger and more expensive terms, fearing that a small fleet might not achieve its objective. It was not therefore until 1560, six months later, that the fleet occupied the island of Djerba as a prelude to Tripoli. However, Dragut, leader of the Barbary corsairs, was lying in wait and, in a surprise attack, captured 10,000 men and eight galleys, as well as the island, in May 1560. This disaster struck home. Philip's reputation had to be restored, but this could only be done with an enlarged navy, and this would not be ready until 1564. Meanwhile, further Turkish raids occurred. Sometimes the corsairs operated on their own – as at la Harradura in 1561, when Dragut sank seven galleys; occasionally they acted in consort with the Porte when, for example, Orán was assailed in 1563. Fortunately for Philip, the Turks only attacked in strength in 1565, partly due to fears that Persia was preparing to assault their eastern flank and partly due to internal rivalry between Selim and Bayazid, the Sultan's sons, and Ali Pasha, the new Grand Vizier. Better planning and attention to detail brought Philip success in 1564 when thirty-three galleys launched an attack on Morocco and recaptured Peñón de Vélez. The King was elated, declaring, 'El Papa esta a la mira' (The Pope is watching us).

From 1560 to 1565 the Knights of St John had launched counter-attacks from Malta against Ottoman ships and the Barbary coast. Retaliation was inevitable and came in May 1565 when 180 Turkish warships besieged their island base (**9**). The Knights held out until September, when Don García de Toledo, Viceroy of Naples, arrived from Sicily and scattered the besiegers. The relief of Malta enhanced Philip's prestige, saved Sicily, and marked the limit of Ottoman influence in the western Mediterranean, but Turkish power was far from extinguished. Each summer Christians held their breath to see where the Turks were next going to strike. In 1570 Venice was the reported target, but instead Algerian troops captured Tunis and threatened la Goletta. Cyprus, a wealthy Venetian colony, was also invaded, and Nicosia and Cyrenia fell in September. As Italians quaked with anticipation, Pius V took the initiative by inviting Spain to join Venice, Genoa and a number of other Italian states, including the Papacy, in a Holy League. Although the Papacy offered to remit Spanish clerical taxes worth 1 million *ducats*, Philip was unenthusiastic. Spain would not be in charge of the campaign, nor even the dominant partner, since Venice would supply most of the ships and troops, and with limited finances he was far more interested in re-capturing Tunis and Algiers than in defending Venice. Even after he had agreed to join the League he gave it so little chance of success that in January 1571 he considered withdrawing, and only decided not to do so because, as he candidly remarked, 'our prestige will certainly suffer if we do not provide what we promised'. Nine months later, at Lepanto in the Gulf of Corinth, a Christian fleet led by Philip's half-brother, Don John of Austria, captured more than half the Turkish ships and killed 30,000 Turks including their admiral, Ali Pasha. The Ottoman fleet had suffered its worst defeat since 1402, and although Philip had only contributed 79 ships he enjoyed the kudos of victory. As Venice celebrated for a week and the Pope ordered a *Te Deum*, Philip commissioned Titian to paint 'Spain Coming to the Aid of Religion' on a particularly large canvas.

Traditionally historians have viewed Lepanto as a seminal event, claiming that after it the Mediterranean no longer held centre stage in Europe, that it ended the long conflict between Muslims and Christians, and marked the beginning of Turkish naval decline (**12, 13, 36, 85**). The extant evidence in the Turkish archives simply does not bear out this retrospective judgement. Selim's response to the defeat was to rebuild his fleet and double his resolve to control North Africa and the sea routes via Malta and Sicily (**58**). Moreover, the Christian victory was not followed up by Spain for a number of reasons. The victors had suffered heavy losses – 8,000 dead, 15,000 wounded and twenty ships lost – and the Venetians were unreliable allies. In addition, Don John was so unpredictable that he might risk and lose everything, and the campaigning season was already well advanced. Finally, Philip believed that the sting in the Turkish tail had only been partially drawn. His caution was justified. Only weeks after Lepanto the Turks captured Cyprus, a salutary reminder that their potential to inflict a serious blow was still formidable. In 1574, 300 galleys led by Euldj Ali recaptured Tunis and la Goletta and threatened Sicily. However, just when it seemed that the Turks were recovering the initiative, Selim died in 1575 and news of the death of the Persian Shah led to a renewal of internecine war in the Middle East.

Since 1575 Philip had taken secret soundings about the possibility of a truce with the Porte. Negotiations were complicated by Portugal's attack on Morocco in 1578, but it was significant that when the flower of the Portuguese nobility was killed at Alcázarquivir, neither Philip nor Murad responded (**58**). Both had serious domestic problems and realised that their Mediterranean conflict was a war neither could win. A truce was concluded in 1578 by Philip's agent in Constantinople, Giovanni Margliani, which served as the basis of a treaty signed in August 1580 and renewed in 1581 for three years. The Venetians felt betrayed, the Pope was mortified, and even the Spanish clergy called for the annulment of the *cruzada** and *excusado**. Philip, however, was unmoved. Unlike his father, he was not a crusader; on the contrary, he saw it to be his Christian duty to reach an honourable peace with the Porte. The benefits were mutual. As the Turks expanded towards the Caspian Sea, engaging the Persians in war between 1578 and 1590 and threatening the Portuguese trade in the Indian Ocean, Philip could again turn his attention to northern Europe and entertain grandiose schemes involving England and France. Nevertheless, if the Ottoman threat to the Iberian possessions had receded in the course of his reign, Spain had lost almost all of her North African outposts. At best Philip's policy had been defiant and honourable, but for the most part he had been on the defensive. The Cross could contain but not expunge the Crescent (**187**).

Portugal

Portugal was ruled by Sebastian I (1557–78), until his ill-fated decision to lead a crusade against the Turks saw his disappearance and assumed death at Alcázarquivir in Morocco. The heir was his great-uncle Henry, a deaf, half-blind, toothless, sixty-six-year-old cardinal who was far from well when he surprisingly married the thirteen-year-old daughter of the Duchess of Bragança. On 31 January 1580 Henry died and a succession dispute erupted (**28**).

Philip was well prepared, having already set up a Portuguese committee in 1579 to facilitate his claim. On paper he was the best male claimant, through his mother Isabella, daughter of Emmanuel I of Portugal, but he was challenged by Don António, an illegitimate son of Henry's brother, and by Catalina, Duchess of Bragança, whose son was in prison in Seville. Philip responded decisively. He sent the Duke of Osuna and Cristóbal de Moura to Lisbon to offer inducements to nobles and influential members of the *Cortes**. He promised to pay the ransom of nobles captured in 1578, and won over the Braganças by granting them land and titles and agreeing to release their son. Lisbon merchants realised that union with Spain would bring commercial advantages, and the Portuguese clergy were prepared to welcome Philip as their new ruler. Only the townspeople remained sceptical and some, fearing Spanish subjugation, found their possible saviour in Don António. By June 1580 supporters had raised his flag in Santarem, Oporto, Lisbon and Sétubal, prompting Spain to invade with 37,000 troops. It was a well-planned and skilfully executed campaign and, although António escaped, his forces were beaten and by August Philip was in control of Portugal (**25**).

Between December 1580 and February 1583 Philip resided in Lisbon and displayed his political wisdom. He wore Portuguese-style clothes, cut his beard according to their fashion and learned their language. In April 1581 the Tomar *Cortes** recognised him as King, and in 1582 he sensibly let the Portuguese retain their own customs, coinage, language and laws. A Council of Portugal was set up, the *Cortes* was to meet as before, and all administrative offices were reserved for nationals. Philip's viceroy was to be Portuguese or a member of the Habsburg royal family; the first was the twenty-three-year-old Archduke Albert of Austria (1583–93) and he was succeeded by leading Portuguese nobles.

The annexation of Portugal brought several advantages to Spain. Her empire comprised Brazil, West Africa, the Spice Islands and the Azores, an important base for the Indies fleet. Her navy contained galleasses as well as galleons and gave Philip greater security in the west of Spain and the opportunity to reach the Netherlands, England and France by sea. Her crown brought Philip enormous prestige. For the first time since the Roman occupation the Iberian peninsula was under one Christian ruler which, in the opinion of Peter Pierson, was 'the greatest triumph of his reign' (**136**, p. 147). Certainly, as ruler of 40 million people he was the most powerful man in the world and, according to his court historian Cabrera Córdoba, it was in the 1580s that he began to call himself 'King of Spain'. But unification also brought problems. Portugal's long Atlantic coastline was vulnerable to attack and a prime target for interlopers in search of the East and West Indies trade ships (**8**). António also continued to plague Philip. In 1582 France assisted him in an abortive attempt to seize the Azores, and the English twice tried to restore him to the Portuguese throne. It was as well for Philip that France and England only regarded him as an ancillary weapon in their war against Spain and that he died in exile in 1595 (see p. 84).

England

Friendship and co-operation 1554–67
Philip's marriage to Mary Tudor in 1554 was not made in heaven but in Brussels by Charles V's councillors. In the summer of 1553, as Charles lay ill, they planned to contain the growing power of France and facilitate Spain's control of the Netherlands in the face

of rival claims from their Austrian cousins, by creating a new northern state out of England and the Netherlands which would be inherited by Philip and Mary's heirs. Philip was not consulted and Mary first heard of the plan from the imperial ambassador in England, Simon Renard (**94, 153**).

Philip visited England on two occasions: from July 1554 to August 1555, and from March to July 1557 when he came to enlist England's support in his war against France. He viewed England as a valuable counterweight to the Guises in France and Scotland that could make a telling contribution at a critical moment in the Habsburg–Valois struggle in northern France. He did his best to court the English by distributing largesse and even drinking beer, but there was evident antipathy towards the Spaniards who were deemed arrogant, aggressive and excessively numerous. Anti-Spanish literature like *A supplicacyon to the Quenes Majestie* and *A warnyng for Englande* heightened the tension. Only with great difficulty did Philip and Mary persuade the Council to agree to go to war with France in 1557. Its reluctance was justified. Once war was declared, Spain refused to break off relations with Scotland, ignored suggestions that the Hanseatic League should have fewer privileges in England, and in the opinion of the Council allowed Calais to be lost. Moreover, Mary was saddened by Philip's lengthy absences and her unrequited love. The Spaniards were equally disenchanted with the English. In Philip's estimation, they were ungrateful, untrustworthy and fractious, had been conspicuous by their absence in the defence of Calais, and contributed next to nothing in the ensuing campaigns.

Philip shed few tears at the death of Mary in November 1558, but he showed concern at the effect it might have on the peace negotiations currently under way at Câteau-Cambrésis. England's alliance must be retained to offset the Guises's influence in Scotland, but Queen Elizabeth flatly refused to acknowledge the loss of Calais. The Spanish ambassador in London, the Duke of Feria, keenly advocated a marriage between Elizabeth and Philip, which seemed to offer benefits to both parties. Elizabeth was regarded as illegitimate by the Papacy and needed Philip's protective arm not only to save her from the missives of the Vatican but also to ward off threats from the ambitious Guises. For his part, the possibility of helping Elizabeth return England to the Catholic faith and frustrating French ambitions in Scotland would more than offset the expected French pique when they discovered he was not going to marry Henry II's daughter. Yet, in truth, Philip did not find Elizabeth Tudor at all attractive, and when he affirmed his offer of marriage in January 1559, he likened his position to that of 'a man under sentence of death'. In fact, she turned him down and he wisely married Elizabeth of Valois instead.

Between 1559 and 1567 Anglo-Spanish relations were sound but never particularly good, because they rested upon personal relationships and mutual opposition to the Guises rather than on trade and marital ties. The Protestant religious settlement of 1559 disturbed Philip, although he took the pragmatic view that it was neither propitious to intervene in English affairs nor wise to jeopardise the goodwill of Elizabeth. 'The evil that is taking place in that kingdom', he informed Feria, 'has caused me the anger and confusion I have mentioned . . . but we must try to remedy it without involving me or any of my vassals in a declaration of war until we have enjoyed the benefits of peace' (**112**, p. 84). He personally persuaded the Papacy not to excommunicate Elizabeth, fearing such an action might trigger off a Catholic revolt in England which France would exploit. Neither a minor trade war in 1563–65 nor the Dutch Revolt disturbed the diplomatic harmony, although much of the cordiality was due to the Spanish ambassador, Guzman de Silva (1564–68), who was popular with the Queen and adept at pouring oil on troubled waters.

Years of estrangement: 1567–85
The year 1567 was a turning-point in Philip's relationship with Elizabeth, the key to which lay in the Netherlands (**35**), (see p. 66). Alva's army was seeking to establish Spanish rule at the expense of Dutch political and religious liberty, and if he succeeded it might encourage Philip to try and regain England for the Catholic faith. Elizabeth had not sufficient military, naval or fiscal strength to stop Alva, but by seizing Spanish silver bound ultimately for the Army of Flanders she could bleed his supply lines. Perhaps the three voyages of John Hawkins to West Africa in the 1560s and the selling of cloth and slaves in Spanish America, forbidden by the Treaty of Tordesillas, were politically as well as commercially inspired (**142**). The Spanish gave an unequivocal reaction when they seized ten of Hawkins' ships at San Juan de Ulúa in September 1567. It was this event which sparked off a wave of anti-Spanish pamphleteering and spawned the English myth that Philip was an agent of evil (**108**).

Elizabeth responded in 1568 by commandeering five Genoese silver ships carrying £40,000 of bullion bound for the Netherlands when they sought refuge from Channel pirates (**182**). The new

Spanish ambassador, De Spès, alerted Alva who imposed an embargo on Anglo-Dutch trade in January. When the Queen retaliated by seizing forty Spanish ships in English waters, Philip ordered all English ships in Spanish ports to be held. Trade was only normalised in 1573 when Elizabeth signed the Convention of Nijmegen and agreed to compensate the Genoese bankers. Although eleven major English expeditions to Spanish America took place between 1572 and 1577, Elizabeth claimed these were unofficial, and she specifically disowned all responsibility for Drake's attack on Nombre de Dios in 1573 and for his lucrative circumnavigation of the globe between 1577 and 1580 (**1**, **2**). Philip had doubts about Elizabeth's innocence, and these were strengthened when he learned in 1584 that Raleigh and Grenville had tried to establish a settlement in Roanoke, Virginia which directly threatened Spanish shipping routes. A decree of 19 May 1585 ordered the confiscation of all English goods and shipping in Iberian waters, but this prompted Elizabeth to issue letters of marque to merchants, allowing them to recuperate any losses they had sustained at Spanish hands by plundering Spanish ships.

Elizabeth also provoked Spain in Europe. First, she financed the Portuguese pretender, Don António, in 1583, and when he was driven out of the Azores gave him temporary exile at her court. Second, and far more damaging, was her intervention in the Netherlands, though this was long delayed. In March 1572 she ordered the expulsion of the Dutch privateer William, Baron of Lumey de la Marck, from Dover, thereby triggering a major uprising in Brill and Flushing, which in effect inaugurated the Dutch war of independence. The Spaniards regarded Elizabeth's action as deliberate provocation, but there is no evidence that she anticipated or influenced the consequences. Indeed, for the next thirteen years she followed Burghley's advice to keep out of involvement in the Netherlands (**105**, **161**, **181**, **184**). It was the deaths of Anjou and William of Orange in 1584 and the fall of Antwerp in 1585, leaving Holland and Zealand exposed, which brought matters to a head. Since Henry III of France showed no desire to challenge Spain, Elizabeth committed herself militarily to the Dutch cause. By the Treaty of Nonsuch, signed on 20 August 1585, she agreed to send £126,000 and 6,000 men under the leadership of the Earl of Leicester to aid the rebels, in return for Flushing, Brill and Rammekens. Leicester and Walsingham were convinced that unless Spain was stopped, England would be next to fall, but there is no extant evidence in the Spanish archives to corroborate their analysis of Philip's intentions.

Elizabeth's attempt to justify this provocative act, expounded in *A Declaration of the Causes Moving the Queen of England to give aid to the Defence of the People afflicted and oppressed in the Lowe Countries*, fooled no one – least of all Philip. Upon hearing in October that Drake had attacked Vigo and Bayona in Galicia, the King took the decision to launch the Armada. English troops had invaded his territory, occupied his fortresses and challenged his sovereignty. They must be removed and his reputation avenged.

The breakdown in Anglo-Spanish relations cannot be attributed solely to Elizabeth, for Philip also acted provocatively. Central to Spain's machinations was Mary, Queen of Scots. In 1568 she had sought political exile in England, but as she had a claim to the throne and was a Catholic, she was put under house arrest. The Pope was outraged and called upon Philip to rescue her, but the King had no wish to antagonise Elizabeth at this time or jeopardise the welfare of English Catholics, and in any case he was not sure that he could trust the judgement of his resident ambassadors, who claimed the country was in a state of incipient rebellion (**116**). In 1569 he only gave moral encouragement to the rebellion of the Northern Earls and to the Munster uprising in Ireland. In 1570 he even reprimanded Pius V for excommunicating Elizabeth without consulting him. Philip's first overt provocative act came in 1571, at the time of the Ridolfi Plot, when he approved the Council of State's recommendation to send a small fleet of warships to gain control of the North Sea and ordered Alva to transport 10,000 troops to help Mary secure the throne. The general seems to have had doubts about the viability of this plan from the outset, but Philip re-affirmed his order in August, even after Ridolfi's arrest. 'I am so keen to achieve the consummation of this enterprise', he informed Alva, 'I am so attached to it in my heart, and I am so convinced that God our saviour must embrace it as his own cause that I cannot be dissuaded from putting it into operation' (**123**, p. 53). Even so, as it became increasingly obvious that the enterprise was doomed to fail, Philip changed his mind and cancelled his orders.

Philip remained uneasy at the growing persecution of Catholic missionaries and Jesuits in England in the 1580s. Although these priests were nominally apolitical, such was their zeal that the possibility of Catholic-inspired plots on the Queen's life could never be ruled out. At one time Philip had opposed the idea of putting Mary Stuart on the English throne, but now he regarded it as a desirable objective. He had hopes that she could become a Spanish puppet, perhaps even 'his agent in a policy for the general unification of

Christendom under Spanish presidency' (**27**, p. 202). In October 1580 Philip despatched a fleet to Smerwick in Ireland and landed 800 Spanish and Italian troops in the hope of instigating a general uprising centred upon Munster. Prompt action by an English naval squadron forced the rebels to surrender and all but fifteen were massacred. Three years later the Throckmorton Plot was hatched, in which Jesuits, Mary and Mendoza, the Spanish ambassador, planned to assassinate Elizabeth and orchestrate a Catholic uprising in preparation for an invasion by the French Guises and Spanish troops. Upon interrogation Mendoza admitted his involvement and Philip's complicity. To Elizabeth, Philip was dangerous and untrustworthy; to Philip, Elizabeth was the Protestant Jezebel who had exhausted his patience. It was his duty as the Most Catholic King to teach her a lesson.

The Armada and its aftermath: 1585–98

Historians are agreed that Philip may have had several aims in sending the Armada but that his prime objective was to stop the English from interfering in the Netherlands. The English navy impeded his control of the sea and without it he would not recover the disobedient Dutch provinces. A projected attack on England would tie down Elizabeth's fleet, commit her to heavy defence expenditure, and possibly bring her to sue for peace. Philip was perhaps mindful of the Venetian ambassador's comment that 'vigorous preparations for war are the surest way to secure favourable terms of peace'. Ideally Philip would have welcomed the conversion of England to Catholicism, and there is no reason to doubt that religion was a genuine motive, even if a secondary one. After all, 180 clerics accompanied the fleet, twenty-four Jesuits waited in Flanders, and Cardinal Allen, an English-born missionary, was ready to take over the spiritual direction of the new Catholic state. Philip instructed Parma in April 1588 that even if the invasion was only partially successful, he must demand toleration for Catholics [**doc. 15**]. But the Armada was not primarily a religious crusade, for Philip was a realist, not a visionary. He doubted the strength of English Catholicism and its potential to rise up in support of an invasion, and there is no evidence that he intended the conquest of England or even believed that it was possible. At best he hoped to secure the south-east, between Margate and London, as a bargaining counter with which to accomplish his more pragmatic objectives of peace, compensation and toleration for English Catholics.

The plan to launch an Armada was first mooted in August 1583 by Santa Cruz, Captain-General of the Ocean Sea. In January 1586 he again outlined his requirements: 560 ships and 94,000 troops would be needed to enable a decoy strike force to attack southern Ireland while the main fleet landed on the south coast of England directly from Lisbon. The total cost was estimated at 3.5 million *ducats*. Parma doubted whether such a task force would be powerful enough to win a sea battle as well as a land battle, and in June suggested an alternative strategy. He would transport 30,000 troops from Bergen-op-Zoom to Margate in eight to twelve hours and march on London. As he would be travelling in light, shallow boats which were vulnerable to attack, Santa Cruz must clear the Channel of enemy ships. Philip found the plan very attractive: it was practicable and would only cost an estimated 150,000 *ducats* a month. Speed and secrecy were of course essential, yet an invasion in 1586 was ruled out since the campaigning season was already well advanced and in early 1587 Philip was still trying to persuade Sixtus V that the contemplated action would benefit religion [**doc. 14**]. News of Mary Stuart's execution finally convinced the Pope, and in July 1587 he agreed to donate 1 million *ducats* but only after 'the army has been put on land' and provided it landed before the end of the year. There is no truth in the claim that Mary's death played a decisive part in actuating Philip, since he had already decided to attack England; but it did enable him to command the moral high ground and secure papal support.

At some stage in 1586, probably in July, the Council of War proposed combining Parma's and Santa Cruz's plans, but no decision was taken until August 1587 when news that Parma had captured Sluys convinced Philip that a Spanish fleet could join the Army of Flanders at Ostend and invade England simultaneously (**163**). To achieve this, the King decided to drop the Irish diversion and to increase the size of the Armada. Parma opposed this hastily amended plan. He disliked its timing, knew that at present he could not exit past Dutch ships at Flushing, and feared that it would leave the Netherlands totally defenceless. Santa Cruz also had objections but of a more personal nature: he wanted sole command, but unfortunately he died in February 1588.

Philip's appointment of the Duke of Medina Sidonia as his new commander has been viewed critically by many historians, although contemporaries were not at all surprised (**60, 91, 115**). Devout, affable, loyal, very rich and the first grandee in Castile, Medina Sidonia would command respect, help pay for the day-to-day costs and follow Philip's instructions to the letter. Although he had never fought at sea, he had military experience and above all was an expert in naval administration and the re-fitting of ships. Philip knew that the Armada must set sail as quickly as possible and believed that Medina Sidonia was the best man to accomplish this (**137, 166**). Medina Sidonia initially turned down the offer of command, on the grounds that he possessed 'neither aptitude, ability, health nor fortune for the expedition' (**39**, p. 101). When Philip ignored his protests, he insisted that he could not set sail until he had more ships, men and supplies. Perhaps he hoped that this ill-fated expedition would be called off. Certainly, when 130 ships carrying 30,000 men did leave Lisbon on 28 May and immediately ran into a storm off the coast of Finisterre, he urged the King to cancel it [**doc. 16**]. Five ships were missing and urgent repairs required. Philip characteristically replied that God wished it to continue. The King may have doubted the outcome but Spain's reputation was in question and the eyes of the world were upon him. 'To leave our fleet bottled up and ineffective', he contended, 'would be a disgrace.'

The administrative organisation which lay behind the Armada was a remarkable achievement which only Spain's bureaucracy and Philip's meticulous eye for detail could have accomplished. He planned everything from the crew's rations to the rules governing their moral conduct, from grand strategy to the precise terms of naval engagement (**152**). As the Armada sailed through the Channel, it was permitted to defend itself but not to initiate any attacks, and Medina Sidonia stuck rigidly to his orders. In the course of nine days only three ships were lost, of which the most celebrated was the *Nuestra Señora del Rosario* due to the recklessness of its captain, Don Pedro de Valdés. The fleet of 122 ships reached Calais on 6 August, yet Parma was 48 km away and unaware of the Armada's arrival until the following day. He needed forty-eight hours to effect his embarkation, but contrary winds delayed his departure, and by the time he was ready the Armada had been scattered by English fireships. Parma kept his men on a war footing until 31 August, but by then he had learned that the Armada had been mauled off the coast of Gravelines, had cut its anchors, and was now at the mercy of wind and weather. Over the next two months one-third of the remaining ships were lost at sea or wrecked off the Scottish and Irish coasts (**72**).

Could the Armada have succeeded? Historians have long argued about its feasibility. Mattingly claimed 'it was a good plan'; Geyl saw it as 'a mad enterprise'; while Fernández-Armesto believed its chances of success were 'evenly balanced' (**39, 48, 115**). Contemporaries were far less confident. Alva always said it would fail; Medina Sidonia and Parma expressed doubts as soon as the plans were modified; and Parisian bookmakers offered odds of 6 to 1 against it surviving the Channel. Philip attributed the Armada's defeat to divine intervention, but sensibly ordered an enquiry. Officially, only Diego Flores de Valdés, the chief nautical adviser, was held responsible. He had advised the abandonment of the *Rosario* and ordered all cables to be cut when fireships entered Calais. Arrested on his return to Spain, he was sentenced to a year's imprisonment in Burgos jail. Yet if one person was to blame, it was Philip. Geoffrey Parker has claimed with some justification that the prime weakness was the King's 'armchair strategy': 'Philip II failed to conquer England, not because of defective supply, but through unsound strategy and faulty tactics' (**126**, p. 29). No definite arrangements had been made for the junction of the Armada and Parma's land forces. Moreover, Santa Cruz had originally called for forty or fifty galleys to accompany the galleons, but only four left Lisbon and none sailed up the Channel, which was, in the opinion of Don Francisco de Bobadilla, a fatal mistake (**17**). The King also knew that in combat his galleons could only fire one salvo and that the fleet was vulnerable to 'low firing' by the English, yet he still informed his admiral that if he had the opportunity he must 'attack and close with them, ready for hand-to-hand combat' (**126**, p. 33). This proved disastrous at Gravelines, and if it had been attempted in the Channel, the Armada would not have reached Calais.

The Armada may have failed but it was not a total failure, and Philip seemed even more determined to succeed. The fleet was rebuilt and included twelve new 1,000-ton galleons christened the 'Twelve Apostles'. Further armadas were planned and two set sail in 1596 and 1597 only to be destroyed by severe gales. Given the logistical difficulties of launching and co-ordinating the largest seaborne army in history and how close it came to fulfilling its objective, the Armada may be seen as 'a Spanish triumph of organization over adverse circumstances' (**39**, p. 11). However, a question-mark now hung over Spain's image of invincibility and some historians regard the defeat as a turning-point in her history (**112**). It weakened Parma's hand in the Netherlands and encouraged the Dutch and English to counter-attack. In 1589 Drake and Norris sailed to Corunna, burned ships in Lisbon and attacked the Azores, and between 1589 and 1598 Elizabeth endorsed over one hundred private expeditions. Attack and counter-attack continued through the 1590s as the war dragged on: Spanish ships assailed Pembroke in 1595 while Howard and Essex sacked Cadiz in 1596. Both Philip and Elizabeth were too proud to admit that they could not win the war or bring themselves to reach a compromise. It required new leaders and a fresh appraisal of their countries' affairs before peace would result in 1604.

Part Three: Assessment

9 How Absolute was Philip II?

The prevailing view in the sixteenth century was that the Spanish monarchy was absolute, even if this was far from true in practice. Royal pageantry and the mystical coronation ceremony hedged the King with a divinity that surpassed popular understanding and, as God's sovereign ruler, he was the supreme law-giver. It was his prerogative to take all decisions, to interpret and when necessary override the laws, which in theory rendered his authority '*ab solutus*', free from control of the laws. Such power was needed for those rare occasions when natural justice required his intervention, but this did not give him the right to flout the law. Like his subjects, Philip was under the rule of divine and natural law, but whereas they had to answer to the King's judges, he was answerable to God alone. Contemporary scholars and jurists like Luis de Molina (d. 1600) and Francisco Suárez (d. 1617) were generally agreed that all men, including the King, were subject to natural law, but that even if the King acted outside the law or imposed unjust laws upon his subjects, it remained their duty to obey him (**55**). Few writers were as radical as Juan de Mariana (d. 1624), whose views anticipated the Social Contract doctrine of the late seventeenth century. He averred that subjects could depose a ruler if it was in their interest to do so since 'the King must be subject to the laws laid down by the state, whose authority is greater than that of the King' (**92**, p. 296) [**doc. 18**]. Such opinions had no place in Philip's philosophy although, of course, this does not necessarily mean that he harboured ideas of becoming an absolute king.

The maintenance and enforcement of law and order was the prime duty of all sixteenth-century monarchs and a bench-mark against which suggestions of royal absolutism may be measured; without justice, government was neither respected nor effective. Philip's strategy was to be resolute and fair, which was in line with his father's advice to impart justice 'in such a manner that the wicked find him terrible and the good find him benign'. Philip inherited a system of hierarchical law courts which appears to have operated impartially and without excessive royal interference (**149**). He established more *audiencias**, codified the Castilian laws in 1567, and did his best to ensure that no favouritism was shown to members of the nobility. For example, in 1582 the Admiral of Castile was arrested on a murder charge, tried, found guilty and executed. The aristocracy were taught that they were not above the law. Indeed, Castillo de Bobadilla could claim in 1597 that Philip had suppressed them so successfully that 'there is no judge now who cannot act against them and take their silver and horses'. Contemporaries certainly regarded Philip as 'the justest of rulers'.

Philip only intervened in the law when he felt that natural justice could be or had been perverted, where his own ministers who were directly answerable to him were concerned, and when the security of the state was threatened. In 1593, for example, he used his prerogative to dispense with the law when he insisted that Toledo convicts who were transferred from serving on galleys to the mercury mines at Almadén must be released as soon as they had served their sentences. 'Although galley labour may be harder than the mine', said Philip, 'it is not my wish that they be harmed' (**51**, p. 94). And a subsequent enquiry into convicts' treatment suggests that his instructions were carried out. Sometimes the crown intervened for reasons which were far from equitable or altruistic, and it is on account of these occasions that charges of absolutism and tyranny have been laid against the King. It was commonplace in all countries for men to be arrested, held indefinitely without trial and tortured. Spanish prisons were full of such victims. Philip was not above the authorisation of state murders, as the deaths of Escobedo and Montigny testify, and an open verdict must remain as to how Don Carlos died (see p. 7).

Rebellion was a sin against God and an act of treason punishable by death, yet the Dutch Revolt produced some of the most vitriolic attacks against Philip, admittedly mainly from Protestant and Dutch writers in defence of the victims. In his *Apology* of 1580 William of Orange condemned Alva's brutality and Philip's despotism, asserting, 'this tyrant ought not to be endured on this earth', an opinion reiterated 300 years later by the American historian J. L. Motley (**118**). Between 1567 and 1573, more than 1,000 people were executed, including Counts Egmont and Hornes. While it is true that customarily Knights of the Order of the Golden Fleece could only be tried by their Chapter, whereas both Egmont and Hornes had been found guilty by a special tribunal, Philip regarded them as rebels in arms. Alva's comment that 'everyone must be made to live in constant fear of the roof breaking down over his head' should be seen therefore in the context of a serious military problem rather than – as one historian has suggested – a 'ghoulish maxim which links sixteenth-century absolutism with twentieth-century dictatorship' (**73**, p. 71). Anyone who betrayed the monarch's trust was dealt with summarily. The Justiciar of Aragon and two of his associates were executed without trial in 1590 as a result of their complicity in a revolt which had directly challenged Philip's authority. 'It is preferable that all take heed from the public punishment of the few,' Philip once said, and there is little doubt that he would have executed Pérez after 1591 if he could have laid hands on him.

Pérez, in his *Relaciones* of 1591, went some way towards adumbrating the Protestant view that Philip was a cruel, murderous, absolute King. The Black Legend*, the belief that in time Spain would subordinate its dominions and deprive its subjects of their freedom, had its origins in fifteenth-century Italy but assumed a more international currency in Philip's reign as first the Dutch and then the English reviled the King (**108**, **163**). Criticisms of Philip even came from the pens of a minority of Spaniards like Iñigo Ibánez de Santa Cruz, who in his *Anatomy of Spain* in 1598 accused him of being 'a great hypocrite, incestuous King, accursed murderer, unjust usurper, detestable tyrant and monster'. Many Protestant historians have concurred. The nineteenth-century historian Robert Watson believed Philip committed 'the most odious and shocking crimes'; J. L. Motley claimed that Spain had been governed 'by an established despotism'; and in 1947 C. J. Cadoux declared that Philip was a 'monstrous tyrant' (**16**, **118**, **179**). In recent years historians have modified their views of Philip's alleged crimes and the myth of the Black Legend has been debunked, but the question of absolutism remains a live issue. In 1971 the Spanish historian A. Domínguez Ortiz claimed that 'royal absolutism was a reality under Philip II', a view shared by Sir Charles Petric and Philip's most recent biographer, Peter Pierson (**33**, p. 10: **133**, **136**). In 1981 John Lynch attempted to square the circle by suggesting that while the monarchy was absolute, 'its absolutism was qualified by conditions and its power was less imposing in practice than it was in theory' (**104**, p. 208).

A more sensible approach to the question of royal power is to view Philip as an autocrat whose principal aim in government was to continue the work of his predecessors in pursuit of greater unity and conformity rather than absolutism (**70**, **159**). In his administration of the Church, he came to control all clerical appointments, disposed of ecclesiastical wealth and mobilised the Inquisition as an instrument of royal authority. In secular affairs, the 1560s saw a reassertion of royal claims to salt deposits, mining rights and customs revenues; Madrid was established as the administrative and political capital and reforms were made to the Council of Finance and *Casa de Contratación**. Above all, there was a restoration of direct royal control over military and naval administration. This increase in centralisation was accompanied by an expansion in the number of crown servants, consisting mainly of nobles seeking to recover or retain their declining political status and middle-class bureaucrats and *letrados** eager to acquire a more elevated social position. Yet both groups hindered the nascent centralised state and worked against the development of royal absolutism, for low salaries and the declining purchasing power of money encouraged dishonesty and incompetence which further diluted the effectiveness of Philip's rule. Thus, even if he had wanted to be absolute, Philip lacked the means to accomplish it. The further from the capital of his Empire, the less effective was his authority. The lack of a centralised administration, or even of a police force, outside Madrid, and the limited strength and efficacy of the standing army, meant that Philip did not have the means to do as he might have liked. Spain under Philip II had achieved, in the words of J. Viçens Vives, 'a maximum concentration of power at the apex and its minimal diffusion towards the base' (**174**, p. 5). The vastness of his possessions and the time required to obtain reliable information – what Braudel called the 'space–time factor' – further reduced the effectiveness of Philip's administration. When in 1590 he ordered his lieutenant in Milan to expel all Jews living in Lombardy, nothing happened. The order was repeated in 1595 and twice again in 1596 with the warning: 'If this is not done at once, it will be necessary to send someone from here to do it.' No one stirred. Finally, in January 1597 Philip threatened to 'seek out and punish whoever has caused these delays' if the expulsion was not effected immediately. And, at last, it was (**123**, p. 194).

In reality the Iberian peninsula consisted of a series of individual autonomous kingdoms, each with its own laws, languages, customs and economic barriers, which would not experience political unity until the eighteenth century and then without the presence of Portugal. Henry Kamen has shown that in the province of Salamanca 63 per cent of the lands were under noble jurisdiction and 6 per cent under Church control, more than half of Catalonia was covered by semi-independent franchises where the King's writ only indirectly reached his subjects, and in Valencia a mere 73 out of 300 towns were under royal control (**70**). The Basque provinces only recognised Philip as their feudal lord; the Navarrese *Cortes** prevented him from imposing taxes on them; and both Aragon and Portugal insisted that he respect their traditional rights, or *fueros**. The Italian parliaments similarly cherished their liberties and only regarded the King of Spain as 'first among equals', while Milan and Naples successfully resisted attempts to introduce the Spanish Inquisition. Finally, Philip's Burgundian subjects amply demonstrated what could happen if their traditional representative assemblies were ignored, and just how far they were prepared to go to defend their concept of sovereignty. Philip had to accept that each kingdom and duchy was at a different stage of political, economic and social evolution and that any attempt to impose his will on them would be vigorously opposed. The King was the only element of union in a loose federation made up of states, each of which regarded him exclusively as its own ruler. Xenophobia ran deep and surfaced at all levels of society: Christians' abhorrence of Moors and Jews, Castilian scorn for Aragonese, and Italian and Flemish resentment of Spanish domination intensified the differences within and between the dominions. Only in Castile was there any degree of centralisation, but even here effective government rested on the co-operation of local elites, town guilds and traditional landowners. I. A. A. Thompson has shown that the onset of continuous war from 1566 put such a tremendous strain on the crown's resources that its centralist policies collapsed and real power passed to the local municipalities (**164**).

Philip exercised a good deal less than total control. In theory his power was unlimited, but it is a historical myth to say that he was an absolute king. Indeed it is probable that he never had any aspirations in that direction at all, although it is easy to see how this judgement has been formed. The size of Spain's Empire, the scale of her resources, the resolute determination of her King, and the state's apparently omniscient and omnipotent administration appeared to contemporaries as the hallmarks of a threatening monolith. In practice, however, Philip's armed forces were insufficient to defend his empire or impose his wishes on this or anyone else's subjects; his administration exercised ineffectual control over the Castilian towns and over the provinces outside Castile; and his annual revenue fell well short of budgetary requirements. As Thompson pertinently suggests: 'Absolute Monarchy is to be judged not by what it looked like but by how it worked' (**164**, p. 286).

10 Success or Failure? Spain in the 1590s

To most contemporary Spaniards, and on balance to most modern historians, Philip was a successful king. Sir Charles Petrie claimed that his main achievements were the banishment of the Turks from the western Mediterranean and the unification of the Iberian peninsula, a feat unparalleled by Charles V (**133**). Helmut Koenigsberger has adopted an equally positive stance towards Philip, suggesting that if Vervins was nothing more than a restoration of Câteau-Cambrésis, at least Spain gained an honourable peace; that if the Armada failed, at least Elizabeth could not afford to leave her subjects undefended nor could she commit huge sums in helping the Dutch; and that if the United Provinces remained disobedient, the southern states were still firmly under Spanish control. Koenigsberger writes:

> Undoubtedly he failed in his highest aims: in the complete reconquest of the Netherlands, in the conquest of England and in the acquisition of the French crown. . . . But there is no evidence that, when he lay on his deathbed, in the summer of 1598, either he or the great majority of his contemporaries thought his reign as a whole had been a failure (**83**, p. 95).

Philip had defended his *monarquía** and his faith by championing the Catholic Counter-Reformation. He had not lost any of his patrimony but had instead expanded his dominions to make the Spanish Empire the largest and richest in the world.

Some historians have been less wholehearted with their praise, arguing that the major reversals in the last quarter of Philip's reign left Spain in a weak and vulnerable position. Peter Pierson believes that the year 1585 was the high-water mark. Portugal was secure; only three of the Netherlands' provinces – Holland, Zealand and Utrecht – were still in revolt; the peace with Turkey was holding; the Indies' wealth continued to pour in; and only England and France were of major concern. Thereafter, however, matters started to go seriously wrong (**136**). Henry Kamen concurs, although he prefers to put the height of Spanish imperialism at 1580 and sees

96

indications of its decline from 1588, when Philip's enterprises proved too extensive for his resources and for his highly personal direction of affairs (**70**). Both historians stress that in the 1590s Spain, like most west European states, was undergoing a serious domestic crisis. Her outward display of dynastic power, material wealth and spiritual fulfilment had only been achieved at enormous costs and masked serious weaknesses. Philip's Empire was far-flung, difficult to administer and defend, and viewed by his non-Castilian subjects as more Spanish than imperial. Portugal, his most recent acquisition, found her trade, shipping and coastline constantly attacked after 1580 and she was paying increasing taxation for the privilege of being ruled by Spain. As seeds of revolt germinated, all eyes were on the 'disobedient' Dutch whose rebellion continued to sap Spain's strength (**19, 74**).

Politically, the state was more centralised by 1598, but administration was interminably slow, inefficient and corrupt. Government ministers were drawn more from the lower ranks than in 1556, but this only served to oblige the crown to appoint the grandees to viceroyalties, military commands and ambassadorships. The King's omniscience had acted like a strait-jacket at all levels of decision making. In 1600, following Philip's death, a grandee claimed acrimoniously that the world 'would see what the Spanish were worth now that they have a free hand, and are no longer subject to a single brain that thought it knew all that could be known and treated everyone else as a blockhead'. Independent thought was equally threatened by the Inquisition, which impeded the free flow of European ideas and tried to control the social, moral and intellectual climate of Spain. If the country was largely free from heresy in 1598, religious uniformity had not been achieved and the Catholic Church was fundamentally unreformed. The Moriscos remained a Trojan horse, Jews were growing in number, and native Spaniards clung tenaciously to their pagan beliefs despite the Tridentine Decrees and the reformed Catholic orders.

Economically, some *arbitristas** believed Spain was already in decline. Plague, famine, depopulation, inflation, declining agriculture and industry, and an adverse balance of trade, were inescapable problems in the 1590s. 'The Kingdom is wasted and destroyed', claimed the *Cortes** in 1594, 'for there is hardly a man in it that enjoys any fortune or credit.' Such a jeremiad may well be overdrawn, but the sentiments behind this *cri de coeur* were sincere. The wealth from the New World continued to flow in, but just as rapidly flowed out, giving Spain the appearance of being enormously rich whereas in reality there was more shadow than substance. The *alcabala** had tripled in Philip's reign, more than one-third of the average Castilian peasant's income was taken away in taxation, and there was a marked growth in poverty at most levels of society. Even the crown, in real terms, was far worse off in 1598 than in 1556.

Any assessment of Philip II assumes the appearance of a paradox. He was rich yet poor, kind but cruel, strong and weak, determined yet irresolute; he recoiled at the sight of blood but was universally condemned as a murderer; a firm upholder of the law, he was seen by many as the archetypal tyrant. Theoretically he possessed enormous power but in practice he was hemmed in by constraints. Having first studied everything in minute detail, he proceeded to execute his designs on a massive scale. Inevitably, his successes and failures ran in tandem; spectacular enterprises yielded monumental results, for it was not in his nature to compromise. As Hugh Trevor-Roper astutely claimed: 'Whenever he made a bid, it was always a shut-out bid' (**168**, p. 57).

Part Four: Documents

A description of Philip II by the Venetian ambassador, Paolo Tiepolo, in 1563

The King was born of the Empress Isabella, daughter of the King of Portugal, on May 21, 1527. He is slight of stature and round-faced, with very pale blue eyes, somewhat prominent lips, and pink skin, but his overall appearance is very attractive. His temperament is very phlegmatic and his condition weak and delicate; he often takes to his bed, sometimes with chest pains and shortness of breath and sometimes, others say, with more serious illnesses. I have heard doctors say that it is unlikely he will live for long. Like other Spaniards he sleeps a great deal; not only does he take a long siesta after dinner, but he does not get out of bed in the morning in any season of the year until two and a half hours before noon. As soon as he rises he hears mass, and then he has little time for anything else before dinner – in fact, usually alone, since he rarely eats with his wife, child, and sister, and others are not considered worthy to be at his table. His meals are very simple, with no more than fifteen different dishes. He eats very little and only safe, substantial foods – hardly any kind of fruit and no fish at all. He dresses very taste-fully, and everything that he does is courteous and gracious. He preserves his kingly dignity, but with all comers he is very natural and cordial – especially by Spanish standards.

J. C. Davis (**31**), pp. 81–2.

Philip II writes to his children, 1582

From 1581 to 1583 Philip was in Lisbon, away from his family, but he main-tained regular contact with his two daughters, Isabella and Catalina. In this letter he describes the safe arrival of a galleon from the East Indies and shows his concern at Prince Diego's health. The boy died later in 1582.

I only know that the ship carried an elephant, which has been sent to your brother by the viceroy whom I sent to the Indies ... who has already arrived there, and he arrived at a good time too because the one who was there already – I mean the viceroy who was there already – was dead. Tell your brother about the elephant, and tell him that I have a book in Portuguese to send him to help him to learn to read the language. It would be very good if he knew how to speak it already. Don Antonio de Castro has come back very pleased with the words the prince said to him in Portuguese – which was very good if he really did say them! This is already a very long letter for someone who is convalescent and weak. God keep you as I desire: your loving father.

L. P. Gachard (**43**), p. 184.

document 3
A practical handbook for *Corregidores*, 1597

Castillo de Bobadilla was a jurist with considerable legal and political experience, having been President of the Council of Castile and corregidor* *for Badajòz, Soria and Guadalajara.*

The *corregidor* is your magistrate and royal official who exercises the greatest jurisdiction throughout the empire in towns and provinces, where doubtful trades are removed, crimes punished and beneficial acts of government enforced. The proof of your authority is the lordship and office which you exercise: it is subject only to the Prince of the Republic. Wherever you rule the judicial functions of all other officials are suspended, all of which is more fully shown in the status and terms of your office. You can enquire into any business even though there are particular magistrates like the Alcaldes de Sacas, Aduanas, Mestas, Hermandad, Prior and Consuls, and others to do this.

Translated from *Política para corregidores*, Book 1, Chapter 2, number 31, cited in (**21**, pp. 223–4).

document 4
Royal instructions for the *corregidor* of Burgos, 1566

In November 1566 the King was anxious for the Castilian Cortes* *to vote him a* servicio* *without delay. Each of eighteen* corregidores* *received* *instructions to secure the appointment of co-operative* procuradores* *who would return to Madrid with sufficient powers to approve a subsidy.*

The King, to
Don Juan Delgadillo, our *corregidor* in the city of Burgos, or your lieutenant.

We have decided to order *Córtes generales* of these kingdoms to be held for the reasons contained in the letter-patent which will be given to you with this letter, and, as you will see from it, we have written to order the chapter and rulers of your city to elect their *procuradores* and give them sufficient power for the business which has to be discussed and concluded there. We order you to have this publicly proclaimed and to order *procuradores* to be elected according to the said letter-patent and according to customary usage; let the *procuradores* be appropriately qualified and be zealous for our service and for the public good of these kingdoms and lordships, and in the election do not permit any canvassing or bribes or the purchase of the position of *procurador* or anything else prohibited by the laws of these kingdoms concerning such matters. According to the custom followed in previous *Cortes*, in order that the proxy granted to the *procuradores* may be suitable and without any defect, a draft of it will be sent with this letter, and similar drafts are being sent to the other cities and towns which have the right to be represented in the *Cortes*, so that all may come in the same way without differences among them. You will ensure, using whatever means you see fit, and removing any difficulty that may arise, that your city grants to its *procuradores* the powers which should be given according to the aforesaid draft, which is in common form, without any limitations or conditions, and that they present themselves by the appointed time, as befits our service; and will advise us of what is done in order to serve us.

Dated Madrid, 6 November 1566. I the King. Authorized by Eraso. Signed by Menchaca y Velasco.

G. Griffiths (**54**), p. 36.

document* 5

The *Cortes*'s petition against new taxes and the crown's reply, 1567

At the conclusion of the 1567 Cortes, *a summary of its petitions and the crown's rejoinder were published in a* Cuaderno *or* Book of Laws, *recorded in this extract by Baltasar de Hinestrosa, chief scribe to the* Cortes. *Petition III was the most contentious issue of a particularly quarrelsome* Cortes.

Philip, by the grace of God, King of Castile, León, Aragón . . . to the most serene prince Charles, our most dear and well-beloved son, and to the princes, prelates, dukes . . . squires, officials and good men, and any other subjects of ours, whatever their status, condition and dignity, of all the cities, towns and villages of our kingdoms and lordships, present and future, and to each and every one of you in your places and authority to whom this letter of ours may be shown, or any copy of it authorized by a public scribe, and anyone of you who may come to know of it in any manner: greetings and favour.

Know that in the *Cortes* which we ordered to be held in the town of Madrid, beginning last year, 1566, and finishing this year, 1567, we were given certain petitions and articles by the *procuradores de Cortes* of the cities and towns of our kingdoms which met together by our command, and we answered these petitions in agreement with our Council. These petitions and articles and our answers were as follows:

THE *CORTES* OF MADRID, 1567
YOUR CATHOLIC ROYAL MAJESTY:

We who have come by Your Majesty's command as *procuradores* to the *Cortes* which you ordered to be celebrated in this town of Madrid, beg Your Majesty in the name of these kingdoms and for the sake of their good government, for the following favours, and we entreat Your Majesty to answer these requests before the *Cortes* is dissolved:

. . . .
PETITION III

Moreover we say that Your Majesty's royal predecessors of glorious memory ordered by laws made in the *Cortes* that no new taxes, imposts, dues or other tributes, particular or general, should be created or collected without the kingdom's meeting in *Cortes* and conceding them, as it says in the law of the ordinance of King Alfonso; but recently, because of certain needs which Your Majesty has incurred, in despite of this order, some new taxes and dues have been created and imposed and others have been increased, such as the taxes on salt, customs, wool, new ports and other things, which have caused such a great shortage of the necessities of life in these kingdoms that very few can now live without great labour, since these new taxes brought greater damage than profit. We beg Your

Majesty therefore to consider this with your usual clemency and to relieve your kingdoms of these new and increased taxes and in future to grant them the favour of keeping the ancient custom as laid down by law, for it is right that, when Your Majesty's subjects have to meet your needs, they should be informed of them and should choose the least inconvenient means of meeting them, and they will certainly do this in accordance with the love and ancient loyalty with which they have served and do serve Your Majesty.

Our answer to this is that, as you already know and have been told many times, because of the great and urgent needs and wars and enterprises which have been confronted by my lord the King-Emperor who is in glory [i.e. Charles V] and by myself in defence of the public cause of religion and Christendom and these kingdoms and our other states, our own patrimony and the ancient royal rents have been so swallowed up that, finding ourselves without any other means of providing what was necessary to maintain our royal state, we have been unable to avoid imposing the methods and the imposed taxes and increases to which you refer in your petition, but when those necessities cease or we find better means of providing for them, we shall be delighted to relieve these kingdoms and to show them in this and in all matters the favour which we wish and which we realise is right. With regard to what you say next, we shall always be pleased in our difficulties to have the advice of the kingdom and to make use of it, since we are certain, as you say, that they will serve us with the same ancient loyalty and love which they have always shown in our service and that of our royal predecessors. With respect to the salt which you mention in your petition among other things, we have annexed to our Crown and royal patrimony the saltings which some knights, councils and other private individuals held in these kingdoms, and we have ordered just compensation to be made for them.

Moreover, we have imposed a tax on the salt which is imported from Portugal, and that exported from Andalucia, and that sold in its saltings, and we have done all this, apart from the aforesaid necessities and causes, using our right as owner, since the salt and its dues belong to us and our Crown and royal patrimony by the laws and ancient right of these kingdoms, and are intended to support the monarchy and its dependants; therefore we have allotted the income from salt to pay for the guards, councils and ministers of justice, and other necessary expenses; but with respect to the price of the salt and the tax, in order to favour these kingdoms, we intend not to have it increase and we shall not increase it, but shall rather order an investigation to be made to see whether the price can be moderated in certain districts and provinces. . . .

And so that all the above may be of public knowledge, we order this *cuaderno* of laws to be publicly proclaimed in this our court so that it may come to the notice of everyone, and no one can plead ignorance; and we order it to be kept and put into execution in our court after fifteen days, and outside our court forty days after its publication.

Given in Madrid, 7 July 1567. I the King. I, Francisco de Eraso, secretary of his royal majesty, had it written by his command. The graduate Diego de Espinosa. The graduate Menchaca. Dr Velasco.

Registered, Martín de Vergara. Martín de Vergara, for the chancellor.

G. Griffiths (**54**), pp. 63–6.

document 6
An *asiento** made between Niccolò Grimaldi and Philip II, 22 May 1558

In 1558 Philip negotiated this asiento *with Grimaldi, a Genoese banker, in Valladolid. The loan of 1 million crowns was accompanied by particularly severe terms, a reflection of the King's financial straits.*

The said Niccolò Grimaldi undertakes to pay in Flanders 800,000 crowns at 72 *grooten* [Flemish groats] per crown, and in the following manner: 300,000 when the first ships arrive from Peru, 250,000 at the end of November and the remaining 250,000 crowns at the end of December of this year 1558. Another 200,000 crowns he undertakes to pay at Milan, at 11 *reals* to the crown, in the course of November and December of this year, half in each month.

His Majesty will repay the said million in Spain at 400 *maravedís* per crown and in the following manner: 300,000 immediately from the money which is at Laredo, 300,000 from the gold and silver arriving by the first ships from Peru and in the event that the payments are not made in October of this year, the said Grimaldi will not be obliged to make his payments at the end of November and December, either in Flanders or in Milan; 300,000 crowns from the *servicios* of Castile in 1559 and bills of exchange without interest will be delivered to him; the remaining 166,666 crowns of the 400 million *maravedís* to be payable in annuities at 10 per cent. He will be repaid

540,000 crowns of outstanding debts as follows: 110,000 in annuities at 10 per cent, 135,000 at 12 per cent, 170,000 at 14 per cent and 125,000 assigned on the mines. The interest on this sum will be reckoned up to the end of 1556 at 14 per cent and for the year 1557 at 8 per cent. He is also granted permission to export 1 million in gold from Spain.

F. Braudel (**12**), pp. 960–1.

document 7

A view of Spain's economic ills in 1600

In his Memorial of 1600, the Valladolid arbitrista*, Martín González de Cellorigo, blamed the economic recession not on inflation but on censos* and juros*.

It is likewise an error to suppose that in good politics the wealth of a kingdom is increased or diminished because the quantity of money in circulation is larger or smaller. Since money is only the instrument of exchange, a small circulation has as good an effect as a large one, or even better, for instead of clogging the wheels of trade and commerce, it makes them run more easily and lightly. . . . *Censos* are the plague and ruin of Spain. For the sweetness of the sure profit from *censos* the merchant leaves his trading, the artisan his employment, the peasant his farming, the shepherd his flock; and the noble sells his lands so as to exchange the one hundred they bring in for the five hundred the *juro* brings. . . . Wealth has been and still is riding upon the wind in the form of papers and contracts, *censos* and bills of exchange, money and silver and gold, instead of in goods that fructify and attract to themselves riches from abroad, thus sustaining our people at home. We see, then, that the reason why there is no money, gold or silver in Spain is because there is too much, and Spain is poor because she is rich. The two things are really contradictory, but although they cannot fittingly be put into a single proposition, yet we must hold them both true in our single kingdom of Spain.

M. Grice-Hutchinson (**52**), p. 144.

document 8

A *Pragmatica** issued by Regent Joanna, 7 September 1558

We order that no bookseller, book merchant or any other person of any state or condition may bring, smuggle, have or sell any book, printed or unpublished work which has been prohibited by the principal office of the Inquisition in whatever language, form or material that constitutes the book, under penalty of death, the loss of all goods and the public burning of the said books.

Translated from V. Pinto Crespo (**140**), p. 97.

document 9

*Concordia** of 1568 restricting the activities of the Inquisition in Valencia

Following complaints by the Cortes* *of Monzon in 1564 that officials and informers were using the Valencian tribunal to protect themselves from the law, a new* Concordia *was issued in 1568 defining its privileges. The Inquisition subsequently appealed to Philip against these revisions and he ordered copies of the* Concordia *to be seized and future printing stopped.*

Article 1: The number of familiars [paid informers] is to be reduced to that provided in 1554, weeding out the least desirable.

Article 2: They must present themselves with their commissions to the local magistrates in order to be entered on the lists without which they forfeit their exemption.

Article 3: In future the servants of officials must really be servants living with them and receiving regular wages in order to be protected by the inquisitors.

Article 4: Inquisitors are not to interfere, at the petition of an official or familiar, with the regulations of the college of surgeons.

Article 5: Outside of cases of heresy, inquisitors must not interfere with the execution of justice by the royal judges under pretext that culprits have committed offences pertaining to them, but in such cases the judges shall be notified and allowed to execute justice, after which the inquisitors can inflict punishment. In case of heresy, however, a prisoner can be demanded, to be returned after trial, provided he is not sentenced to relaxation [i.e. the court could give a more lenient sentence if the accused admitted his guilt].

Article 6: Familiars are not to be protected in the violation of municipal regulations, nor during pestilence, in the refusal to observe the regulations for the avoidance of contagion; they must submit for inspection the goods which they bring in and the royal judges shall not be prevented from imposing the penalties provided in the royal *pragmatíca*.

Article 7: Inquisitors are no longer to defend familiars in matters of the apportionment of irrigating waters, injuries to harvests, vineyards, pastures, forests, furnishing of lights, licences for building, street-cleaning, road-mending and furnishing provisions.

Article 8: Inquisitors are not to publish edicts with excommunication for the discovery of debts, thefts or other hidden offences committed against officials and familiars, nor such edicts against any delinquents save in cases of heresy.

Article 9: Persons arrested, except for heresy, are not to be confined in the secret prison but in the public one, where they can confer with their counsel and procurators, and they are to be allowed to hear mass and receive the sacraments.

Article 10: Inquisitors shall not give safe-conducts to persons outlawed or banished by the royal judges, except in cases of faith [heresy] and then only for the time necessary to appear before them.

H. C. Lea (**89**), vol. 1, pp. 443–4.

document 10
Philip II's anger is vented against the Pope, 1589

Nothing has surprised me more than to see Your Holiness, after an act inspired by God [the Bull against Henry IV] leaving time to the heretics to take root in France, without even ordering that the Catholic partisans of 'the Béarnais' [i.e. Henry IV] should separate from his cause. The Church is on the eve of losing one of its members; Christendom is on the point of being set on fire by the united heretics; Italy runs the greatest danger, and in the presence of the enemy we look on and we temporise! And the blame is put upon me because, looking at those interests as if they were my own, I hasten to Your Holiness as to a father whom I love and respect, and as a good son remind him of the duties of the Holy See! By God's mercy, where have you found in the whole course of my life reasons for thinking of me as you tell me men think of me, and by what right do you tell it me? God and the whole world know my love for the Holy See, and nothing will ever make me deviate from it, not even Your Holiness by the great injustice you do me in writing such things to me. But the greater my devotion the less I shall consent to your failing in your duty towards God and towards the Church, who have given you the means of acting; and, at the risk of being importunate to Your Holiness and displeasing you, I shall insist on your setting to the task.

Letter to Pope Sixtus V, 1589, J. Lynch (**104**), pp. 285–6.

document 11
Maltreatment of Moriscos* in Granada, 1569

A report written in 1569 to Philip II's secretary, Gabriel de Zayas, by Frances de Álava, Spanish ambassador in Paris, after his visit to Granada

I was utterly shocked to see that the priests did not treat those people in the gentle way they should have done; I frequently witnessed the clergy turning around in the very middle of the consecration, between the host and the chalice, to see if the Moriscos and their women were on their knees, and from that position subjecting them to such horrifying and arrogant abuse, a thing so contrary to the worship of God, that my blood ran cold; and after mass the priests would walk through the town with an attitude of menacing contempt towards the Moriscos.

Cited in H. Kamen (**66**), p. 209.

document 12
An extract from William of Orange's *Apology*, 1580

In March 1580 Philip outlawed William, declaring him to be a traitor. Orange replied with his Apology *in which he defended his views and actions and launched a vitriolic attack on Spain in general and Philip in particular, charging him with being a tyrant and a murderer.*

For there is not, I am persuaded, a nation or prince in Europe, by whom it will not be thought dishonourable and barbarous, thus publicly to authorise and encourage murder; except the Spaniards, and their King, who have long been estranged from every sentiment of honour and humanity. In having recourse to private assassinations against a declared and open enemy, does not this mighty monarch confess his despair of being able to subdue me by force of arms?

Cited in J. C. Rule and J. J. TePaske (**157**), p. 9.

document 13

Philip II's concern at the growth of Huguenotism in France, 15 July 1562

About the affairs of France there is nothing more to say . . . except that they are causing me as much concern as is to be expected, seeing the way things are going, both in the matter of the service of God and in everything else; and therefore I cannot omit to help the Catholics although the expense is coming at a very bad time . . . for it seems to me certain that neither the service of God, which is the most important service, nor my own and the welfare of my states will allow me to neglect helping the Catholics. I know well that something will be risked in this, but certainly much more will be risked in allowing the heretics to prevail, for if they do, we may be certain that all their endeavours will be directed against me and my states, so that they will be like them: a result which I will never accept nor overlook, even if it should cost me a hundred lives, if I had them.

Letter to Margaret of Parma, L. P. Gachard (**42**), pp. lxii–lxiii.

document 14

Diplomatic manoeuvres preparatory to the Spanish Armada, 1587

Having gained the Pope's blessing to invade England, Philip was anxious to secure a gift of 1 million ducats and papal approval in support of his claim to the English throne without appearing to be an imperialist. He instructed his ambassador in Rome accordingly.

You will cautiously approach his Holiness, and in such terms as you think fit endeavour to obtain from him a second brief declaring that, failing the Queen of Scotland, the right to the English crown falls to me. My claim, as you are aware, rests upon my descent from the

House of Lancaster, and upon the will made by the Queen of Scotland, and mentioned in a letter from her of which the copy is enclosed herewith. You will impress upon his Holiness that I cannot undertake a war in England for the purpose merely of placing upon that throne a young heretic like the King of Scotland who, indeed, is by his heresy incapacitated to succeed. His Holiness must, however, be assured that I have no intention of adding England to my dominions, but to settle the crown upon my daughter the Infanta.

Letter to the Marquis de Olivares, 11 February 1587, S. Usherwood (**172**), pp. 26–7.

document 15
Philip II outlines the Armada's objectives, 1588

If the Armada succeeds, either by means of fighting or in consequence of the unreadiness of the enemy, you will, when the forces from here have arrived to assure your passage across, go over in God's name and carry out the task assigned to you.

But if (which God forbid) the result be not so prosperous that our arms shall be able to settle matters, nor, on the other hand, so contrary that the enemy shall be relieved of anxiety on our account (which God, surely, will not permit) and affairs be so counterbalanced that peace may not be altogether undesirable, you will endeavour to avail yourself as much as possible of the prestige of the Armada and other circumstances, bearing in mind that, in addition to the ordinary conditions which are usually inserted in treaties of peace, there are three principal points upon which you must fix your attention.

The first is that in England the free use and exercise of our holy Catholic faith shall be permitted to all Catholics, native and foreign, and that those who are in exile shall be permitted to return. The second is that all the places in my Netherlands which the English hold shall be restored to me; and the third is that they [the English] shall recompense me for the injury they have done to me, my dominions, and my subjects, which will amount to an exceedingly great sum.

With regard to the free exercise of Catholicism, you may point out to them that since freedom of worship is allowed to the Huguenots in France, there will be no sacrifice of dignity in allowing the same privilege to Catholics in England. If they retort that I do not allow the same toleration in Flanders as exists in France, you may tell them that their country is in a different position, and point out to them how conducive to their tranquillity it would be to satisfy the Catholics in this way, and how largely it would increase the trade of England and their profits, since, as soon as toleration was brought about, people from all Christendom would flock thither in the assurance of safety.

If the principal design should fall through, it would be very influential in bringing them to these, or the best conditions possible, if the Armada were to take possession of the Isle of Wight. If this be once captured, it would be held, and would afford a shelter for the Armada, whilst the possession of it would enable us to hold our own against the enemy. This matter has also been laid before the Duke [Medina Sidonia], so that in case of failure, and if nothing else can be done, you may jointly with him discuss and decide with regard to it.

The King

Letter to the Duke of Parma, April 1588, S. Usherwood (**172**), pp. 70–1.

document 16
Medina Sidonia implores Philip to postpone the Armada, 24 June 1588

Having experienced severe storms which dispersed the Armada within a few days of setting sail, and sensing that the expedition was ill-fated, Medina Sidonia wrote to the King from Corunna urging him to call it off.

To undertake so great a task with forces equal to those of the enemy would be inadvisable, but to do so with an inferior force, as ours is now, with our men lacking in experience, would be still more unwise. I am bound to confess that I see very few, or hardly any, of those on the Armada with any knowledge of or ability to perform the duties entrusted to them. I have tested and watched this point very carefully, and your Majesty may believe me when I assure you that we are very weak. . . . The opportunity might be taken, and the difficulties avoided, by making some honourable terms with the enemy. Your Majesty's necessities also make it desirable that you should ponder beforehand what you are undertaking, with so many envious rivals of your greatness.

Letter cited in C. Martin and G. Parker (**112**), p. 191.

document 17

A Spanish opinion why the Armada failed

Don Francisco de Bobadilla was the general in charge of the Armada's military on board the San Martín. *When he wrote this letter on 20 August 1588 from somewhere in the North Sea, he expressed his own theories why the Armada had failed to rendezvous with Parma's army.*

I don't know who had the idea that we could join forces in a place with such powerful currents, with a shore so open and liable to cross-winds, and with so many sandbanks. . . . But I believe it is impossible to control all the things that must be concerted at the same time, in order to bring together forces that are so separated, unless one has a different sort of ship from those we brought, in the place we were instructed to join.

Letter to Don Juan de Idiáquez, C. Martin and G. Parker (**112**), p. 268.

document 18

The power of kings and their subjects: a contemporary view

Juan de Mariana (1535–1624) was a Jesuit historian who expounded his views on royal authority in De Rege et Regis Institutione *in 1599. Intended as a guide for Philip III, the treatise maintained that the King must respect the fundamental laws of the land. If he did not, the people could depose him.*

The regal power, if it is lawful, ever has its source from the citizens; by their grant the first kings were placed in each state on the seat of supreme authority. That authority they hedged about with laws and obligations, lest it puff itself up too much, run riot, result in the ruin of the subjects, and degenerate into tyranny. . . . The authority of the commonwealth is greater than that of the kings. Otherwise how would it be possible, unless it were greater, to restrain the power of the kings and to resist their will?

    Kings will be permitted when circumstances require to ask for new laws, and to interpret and lessen the severity of old ones; to make adequate provision, if any eventuality is not covered by the law. However, the king should believe that it is the distinguishing mark of a tyrant to lack reverence for the customs and institutions of the fathers, to overturn the laws at his own whim, to refer to his own licence and convenience everything that he does. Nor is it consistent that lawful princes so conduct themselves that they seem to possess and use a power untrammelled by law.

Since indeed divine and human law and right are expressed by the laws in every phase of life, it is unavoidable that he who violates the laws thereby departs from justice and uprightness. What is conceded to no one is permitted still less to the king.

From Juan de Mariana, *De Rege et Regis Institutione*, I, cited by G. Lewy (**92**).

Genealogy: Philip II's Family

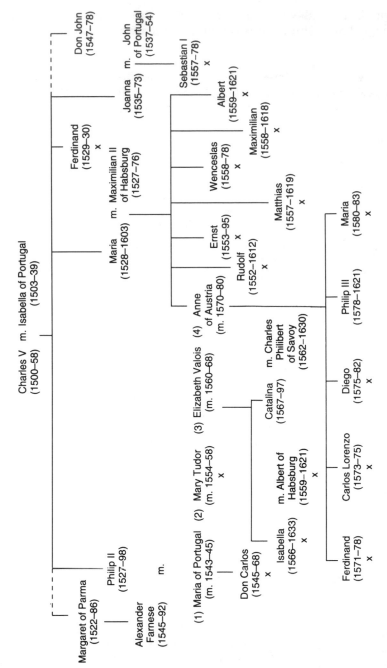

Note: A broken line --- denotes illegitimacy; x = died without issue.

Glossary

Alcabala   A 10 per-cent sales tax.

Alcalde mayor   A chief magistrate.

Almojarifazgos de Indias   Customs duties from the Indies trade.

Almojarifazgos major   Customs duties collected in Seville.

Arbitrista   A writer who drew up *arbitrios* or recommendations for economic and political reform.

Armada del Mar Océano   Created in the 1580s, comprising 106 ships in 1587 which patrolled the Atlantic, the fleet was rebuilt after the Armada, named the Armada of the Ocean Sea in 1594 and by 1598 totalled 67 ships.

Asentista   The holder of an *asiento* (see below).

Asiento   A contract or bill of exchange between the crown and financiers which enabled them to recover their cash at a set time and place and at interest rates that increased according to demand.

Audiencia   A Castilian high court of appeal.

Auto de fé   A ceremony or 'act of faith' at which penitents were encouraged by the Inquisition to abjure their beliefs before receiving sentence. Only a minority of convicted heretics were burned at the stake.

Baldíos   Common land technically owned by the crown.

Black Legend   'La Leyenda negra': the belief which began in Italy in the late fifteenth century and spread to the Netherlands and England in Philip's reign that Spain wanted to rule the world.

Bracci   Parliamentary estates in the non-Castilian Spanish dominions.

Caridades   Feast days when entire communities took a vow to secure protection against evil forces.

Glossary

Casa de Contratación A House of Trade established in 1503 which controlled all vessels, commerce and passengers travelling between Spain and America.

Censo An annuity drawn from loans made to the crown.

Concordia An agreement.

Consejo de Hacienda The Council of Finance.

Consignación The consigning of revenue to finance specific aspects of state expenditure, especially in the navy and army.

Consulado de Mar A body of merchants in Burgos who exercised a monopoly of Castilian trade with the Low Countries and Italy from 1494. A similar monopoly was later granted to Bilbao and Seville.

Consulta Summary of a Council meeting forwarded to the King for consideration.

Contador An accountant or purser in the armed forces.

Contaduría de Hacienda The Treasury's accounting office where taxes were collected and administered.

Contaduría Mayor de Cuentas The principal accounting office.

Conversos Originally Jews who were converted to Christianity, but from the sixteenth century it could also apply to converted Moors.

Corregidor One of sixty-six crown representatives serving the major Castilian towns in a judicial, administrative and political capacity.

Cortes An assembly in each of the Iberian states convened by the crown usually to approve a subsidy. After 1538, the Castilian *Cortes* consisted of one Estate representing eighteen towns and cities. The Aragonese *Cortes* consisted of four Estates and met less frequently.

Cruzada Papal subsidy originally granted to finance Spain's war with the infidel.

Cuaderno A statute or law.

Diputación A committee of eight representatives from the Aragonese Estates which had the power to meet independently of the *Cortes*.

Donativo Money given by the nobles and clergy to the crown upon request; it was also a subsidy voted by the parliaments of Naples and Sicily.

116

Encabezamiento A tax approved by a region which determined its assessment and method of collection.

Erasmianism The ideas of Erasmus, a Dutch humanist, who had exposed clerical abuses and urged the Catholic Church to reform them; the best-known Spanish humanist was Juan Luis Vives.

Excusado A tax on clerical property introduced in 1567 and usually paid as a lump sum by the Church.

Flota A fleet carrying bullion from the Indies to Seville.

Fueros Laws and privileges of the non-Castilian Spanish provinces.

Hidalguía The lowest level of noble status, eagerly sought after as it exempted the *hidalgo* from taxation.

Illuminists 'Enlightened' mystics, also known as *alumbrados*, who re-assessed the Catholic faith and rejected those aspects which they could not uphold.

Index A list of prohibited works (670 in 1559) which was enlarged to more than 2,500 books in 1583–84.

Inquisition An organisation established in 1478 in Castile by papal decree to extirpate heresy and ensure that *conversos* conformed to the Catholic faith. In Philip's reign it investigated all suspected heresies and unchristian activities. The crown had full jurisdiction over the 21 tribunals in the *monarquía*.

Junta A small committee of advisers formed *c.* 1585. The most important was the *Junta de Noche*, which met in the evening until it was superseded by the *Junta de Gobierno* (Governing Committee).

Juraduría A royal councillor.

Juros Credit bonds paid annually to crown bankers out of state revenue. These increased the crown's debts and provided an attractive form of public investment.

Justiciar Aragonese law officer in charge of courts and justice, appointed by the crown for life.

Letrado A lawyer.

Limpieza de sangre 'Purity of blood'. This reflects the concern that Spaniards must be free of Jewish blood, but it was not a controversial issue in Philip's reign.

Glossary

Maestrazgos   There were three Castilian Military Orders or *Maestrazgos* – Santiago, Calatrava and Alcántara – which had been vested in the crown since 1523.

Marrano   A christianised Jew.

Mayor domo   Majordomo or steward of the royal household.

Medio general   The conversion of crown debts into *juros*.

Mesta   A sheepowners' guild established in 1273 to control the three royal sheepwalks or *cañadas* between Barcelona and Navarre; Valencia and Medina del Campo; Málaga/Alicante and Seville.

Millones   An indirect excise tax introduced in 1590.

Monarquía   The dominions of the Spanish crown.

Morisco   A Moor who had been converted to Christianity.

Mudéjar   A Muslim living in Christian Spain. Officially after January 1526 all *Mudéjares* became *Moriscos*.

País   A country or region.

Pechero   An ordinary taxpayer.

Pensiones   A clerical tax on episcopal income.

Placards   Edicts against heretical faiths and practices.

Pragmatíca   A decree.

Procurador   One of thirty-six delegates in the Castilian *Cortes* elected or chosen to represent the eighteen towns of Ávila, Burgos, Córdoba, Cuenca, Granada, Guadalajara, Jaén, León, Madrid, Murcia, Salamanca, Segovia, Seville, Soria, Toledo, Toro, Valladolid and Zamora.

Puertos secos   Castilian customs duties collected at the borders with Aragon, Navarre and Portugal.

Quintal   A weight of just over 100 lbs.

Quinto   20 per-cent duty levied on all American taxes, customs duties and minerals, especially gold and silver.

Reconquista   The 'Reconquest' by which the Moors were expelled from Spain; it began in the eleventh century and ended in 1492 with the capture of the last Moorish state of Granada.

Regidores   Town councillors.

Relaciones   Analyses or accounts of events.

Salinas   A tax on salt.

Seda de Granada   A tax on Granadan silk.

Señorío   A lordship or sovereignty over an area of land or community.

Servicio   A 'service' or grant of taxation made by the *Cortes*. The ordinary *servicio* was payable over three years and an extraordinary *servicio* payable at once.

Servicio y montazgo   A tax on flocks of sheep.

Sisa   A tax on food, first introduced in 1596.

Stadholders   Military and political leaders of the Dutch States appointed by the crown.

States-General   A general parliament of the Netherlands, convened by the Regent or Governor-General in Brussels, and attended by delegates from the seventeen states. All proposals had to be unanimously approved by the delegates, who first had to consult their local assemblies (*staten*).

Subsidio   A clerical tax introduced in 1519 and regularly levied after 1561.

Suprema   *The Consejo de la Suprema y General Inquisición* was a royal council established in 1483 to supervise the inquisitions throughout the Spanish *monarquía*.

Tercias   Church tithes payable to the crown and usually assessed and collected with the *alcabala* as a lump sum.

Tercios   The Spanish infantry.

Bibliography

The place of publication is London, unless otherwise stated.

1 Adams, S., *The Armada Campaign of 1588*, Historical Association, New Appreciations in History, 13, 1988.
2 Andrews, K. R., *Drake's Voyages*, 1967.
3 Basas Fernández, M., *El Consulado de Burgos en el siglo XVI*, Madrid, 1963.
4 Bennassar, P., *Un siècle d'or espagnol*, Paris, 1982.
5 Bennassar, P., *L'Inquisition espagnole, XV–XVI siècles*, Paris, 1979.
6 Bennassar, P., *Valladolid au siècle d'or*, Paris, 1967.
7 Bossy, J., *Christianity in the West, 1400–1700*, Oxford, 1985.
8 Boxer, C. R., *From Lisbon to Goa, 1500–1750: Studies in Portuguese Maritime Expansion*, 1984.
9 Bradford, E., *The Great Siege: Malta 1565*, 1961.
10 Brandi, K., *The Emperor Charles V*, 1939.
11 Bratli, C. G., *Philippe II, roi d'Espagne*, Paris, 1912.
12 Braudel, F., *The Mediterranean and the Mediterranean World in the Age of Philip II*, 1972.
13 Brice, K., 'Philip II: the Mediterranean', in J. Lotherington (ed.), *Years of Renewal: European History, 1470–1600*, 1988.
14 Bujanda, J. M. de, *Index de l'Inquisition Espagnole*, Geneva, 1984.
15 Cabrera de Córdoba, L., *Felipe Segundo, Rey de España*, 4 vols, Madrid, 1876.
16 Cadoux, C. J., *Philip of Spain and the Netherlands*, 1947.
17 Carande, R., *Carlos V y sus banqueros*, vol. i, Madrid, 1943.
18 Casey, J., *The Kingdom of Valencia in the Seventeenth Century*, Cambridge, 1979.
19 Casey, J., 'Spain: A Failed Transition', in P. Clark (ed.), *The European Crisis of the 1590s*, 1985.
20 Chacón Jiménez, F., *Murcia en la centuria del quinientos*, Murcia, 1980.
21 Chamberlain, R. S., 'The *Corregidor* in Castile in the Sixteenth

Century and the *Residencia* as Applied to the *Corregidor'*, *Hispanic American Historical Review*, 23, 1943.
22 Chaunu, H. and P., *Séville et l'Atlantique, 1504–1650*, vol. viii, Paris, 1959.
23 Christian, W. A., *Local Religion in Sixteenth Century Spain*, Princeton, NJ, 1981.
24 Cipolla, C. M., (ed.), *The Fontana Economic History of Europe*, 1974.
25 Clissold, S., 'The Shotgun Marriage: Spain's Annexation of Portugal, 1580', *History Today*, 1980.
26 Contreras, J., 'La Inquisición de Aragón: estructura e oposición 1550–1700', *Estudios de Historia Social*, i, Madrid, 1977.
27 Crowson, P., *Tudor Foreign Policy*, 1973.
28 Danvila, A., *Felipe II y la sucesión de Portugal*, Madrid, 1956.
29 Davies, C. S. L., 'England and the French War, 1557–59' in J. Loach and R. Tittler (eds), *The Mid-Tudor Policy, c. 1540–1560*, 1980.
30 Davies, R. T., *The Golden Century of Spain, 1501–1621*, 1937.
31 Davis, J. C., (ed.), *Pursuit of Power: Venetian Ambassadors – Reports on Spain, Turkey and France in the Age of Philip II, 1560–1600*, New York, 1970.
32 Dedieu, J. P., 'Les causes de foi de l'Inquisition de Tolède (1483–1820)', *Mélanges de la Casa de Velázquez*, 14, Paris, 1978.
33 Domínguez Ortiz, A., *The Golden Age of Spain, 1516–1659*, 1971.
34 Domínguez Ortiz, A., and Vincent, B., *Historia de los Moriscos*, Madrid, 1978.
35 Doran, S., *England and Europe, 1485–1603*, Seminar Studies in History, London and New York, 1986.
36 Elliott, J. H., *Imperial Spain, 1469–1716*, 1963.
37 Elliott, J. H., *Spain and its World, 1500–1700*, New Haven, Conn, 1989.
38 Fernández Alvarez, M., *La política mundial de Carlos V y Felipe II*, Madrid, 1966.
39 Fernández-Armesto, F., *The Spanish Armada*, Oxford, 1988.
40 Fichtner, P. S., *Ferdinand I of Austria*, 1982.
41 Fortea Pérez, J. I., *Córdoba en el Siglo XVI, las bases demográficas y económicas de una expansión urbana*, Córdoba, 1981.
42 Gachard, L. P., (ed.), *Correspondance de Marguerite d'Autriche, duchesse de Parme, avec Philippe II*, vol ii, Brussels, 1870.
43 Gachard, L. P., (ed.), *Lettres de Philippe II à ses filles, les infantes*

Isabelle et Catherine écrites pendant son Voyage en Portugal (1581–83), Paris, 1884.

44 García Carcel, R., *Herejía y sociedad en siglo XVI. La Inquisición en Valencia 1530–1609*, Barcelona, 1980.

45 García Sanz, A., *Desarrollo y Crisis del Antiguo Régimen en Castilla la Vieja. Economía y Sociedad en Tierras de Segovia, 1500–1814*, Madrid, 1977.

46 García Martínez, S., *Bandolerismo, pirateria y control de moriscos en Valencia durante el reinado de Felipe II*, Valencia, 1977.

47 Gentil da Silva, J., *En Espagne: développement économique, subsistance, déclin*, Paris, 1965.

48 Geyl, P., *The Revolt of the Netherlands, 1555–1609*, 1958.

49 González Alonso, B., *El corregidor castellano 1348–1808*, Madrid, 1970.

50 Goodman, D. C., 'Philip II's Patronage of Science and Engineering', *British Journal for the History of Science*, 16, 1983.

51 Goodman, D. C., *Power and Penury: Government, Technology and Science in Philip II's Spain*, Cambridge, 1988.

52 Grice-Hutchinson, M., *Early Economic Thought in Spain, 1177–1740*, 1978.

53 Grierson, E., *King of Two Worlds: Philip II of Spain*, 1974.

54 Griffiths, G., (ed.), *Representative Government in Western Europe in the Sixteenth Century*, Oxford, 1968.

55 Hamilton, B., *Political Thought in Sixteenth-Century Spain*, Oxford, 1963.

56 Hamilton, E. J., *American Treasure and the Price Revolution in Spain, 1501–1650*, Cambridge, Mass., 1934.

57 Hess, A. C., 'The Moriscos: An Ottoman Fifth Column in Sixteenth Century Spain', *American Historical Review*, 74, 1968.

58 Hess, A. C., 'The Battle of Lepanto and its Place in Mediterranean History', *Past and Present*, 57, 1972.

59 Hess, A. C., *The Forgotten Frontier: A History of the Sixteenth-Century Ibero-African Frontier*, Chicago, 1978.

60 Hume, M. A. S., *The Year After the Armada*, 1896.

61 Iongh, J. de, *Mary of Hungary: Second Regent of the Netherlands*, 1954.

62 Jago, C., 'Habsburg Absolutism and the Cortes of Castile', *American Historical Review*, 86 (2), 1981.

63 Jago, C., 'Philip II and the Cortes of Castile: the Case of the Cortes of 1576', *Past and Present*, 109, 1985.

64 Jedin, H., *The Council of Trent*, 2 vols, 1957 and 1961.

65 Kagan, R. L., 'Universities in Castile, 1550–1700', *Past and Present*, 49, 1970.

66 Kamen, H., 'Clerical Violence in a Catholic Society: the Hispanic World, 1450–1720', *Studies in Church History*, 20, 1983.

67 Kamen, H., 'Early Modern Spain: the Difficulties of Empire', *History Sixth*, 2, 1988.

68 Kamen, H., *European Society, 1500–1700*, 1984.

69 Kamen, H., *Inquisition and Society in Spain in the Sixteenth and Seventeenth Centuries*, 1984.

70 Kamen, H., *Spain, 1469–1714: A Society in Conflict*, 1983.

71 Kamen, H., *Golden Age Spain*, 1988.

72 Kemp, P., *The Campaign of the Spanish Armada*, 1988.

73 Kiernan, V. G., *State and Society in Europe, 1550–1650*, 1980.

74 Kilsby, J., *Spain: Rise and Decline, 1474–1643*, 1987.

75 Klein, J., *The Mesta: A Study in Spanish Economic History, 1273–1836*, Cambridge, Mass., 1920.

76 Knecht, R. J., *The French Wars of Religion, 1559–1598*. Seminar Studies in History, London and New York, 1989.

77 Koenigsberger, H. G., *Estates and Revolutions: Essays in Early Modern History*, New York, 1971.

78 Koenigsberger, H. G., *The Government of Sicily under Philip II of Spain*, 1959.

79 Koenigsberger, H. G., *The Habsburgs and Europe, 1516–1660*, Ithaca, NY, 1971.

80 Koenigsberger, H. G., 'The Empire of Charles V in Europe', in *The New Cambridge Modern History*, vol. ii, Cambridge, 1983.

81 Koenigsberger, H. G., 'Western Europe and the Power of Spain', in *The New Cambridge Modern History*, vol. iii, Cambridge, 1968.

82 Koenigsberger, H. G., 'National Consciousness in Early Modern Spain', in *Politicians and Virtuosi: Essays in Early Modern History*, 1986.

83 Koenigsberger, H. G., 'The Statecraft of Philip II', in *Politicians and Virtuosi: Essays in Early Modern History*, 1986.

84 Koenigsberger, H. G., 'Orange, Granvelle and Philip II', in *Politicians and Virtuosi: Essays in Early Modern History*, 1986.

85 Koenigsberger, H. G. and Mosse, G. L., *Europe in the Sixteenth Century*, 1968.

86 Kubler, G., *Building the Escorial*, Princeton, NJ, 1982.

87 Lagomarsino, P. D., 'Court Factions and the Formation of

Bibliography

Spanish Policy towards the Netherlands, 1559–67', Cambridge University Ph.D. thesis, 2 vols, 1973.
88   Lapeyre, H., *Une famille de marchands, les Ruiz. Contribution à l'étude du commerce entre la France et l'Espagne au temps de Philippe II*, Paris, 1955.
89   Lea, H. C., *A History of the Inquisition of Spain*, 4 vols, 1906–7.
90   Lea, H. C., *The Moriscos of Spain*, 1901.
91   Lewis, M., *The Spanish Armada*, 1960.
92   Lewy, G., *Constitutionalism and Statecraft during the Golden Age of Spain*, Geneva, 1960.
93   Limm, P. R., *The Dutch Revolt 1559–1648*, Seminar Studies in History, London and New York, 1989.
94   Loades, D. M., *The Reign of Mary Tudor: Politics, Government and Religion in England, 1553–58*, 1979.
95   Lorenzo Sanz, E., *Comercio de España con América en la época de Felipe II*, vol. 2, 2nd edition, Valladolid, 1986.
96   Lotherington, J., (ed.), *Years of Renewal: European History, 1430–1600*, 1988.
97   Lovett, A. W., *Early Habsburg Spain, 1517–1598*, Oxford, 1986.
98   Lovett, A. W., *Philip II and Mateo Vázquez de Leca: The Government of Spain, 1572–92*, Geneva, 1977.
99   Lovett, A. W., 'The governorship of Don Luis de Requesens, 1573–76. A Spanish view', *European Studies Review*, 3, 1972.
100 Lovett, A. W., 'Juan de Ovando and the Council of Finance (1573–75)', *Historical Journal*, xv, 1972.
101 Lovett, A. W., 'The Castilian Bankruptcy of 1575', *Historical Journal*. xxiii, 1980.
102 Lovett, A. W., 'The General Settlement of 1577', *Historical Journal*, xxv, 1982.
103 Lynch, J., 'Philip II and the Papacy', *Transactions of the Royal Historical Society*, 5th series II, 1961.
104 Lynch, J., *Spain Under the Habsburgs*, vol. 1, Oxford, 1981.
105 MacCaffrey, W. T., *Queen Elizabeth and the Making of Policy, 1572–88*, Princeton, NJ, 1981.
106 Mackay, A., *Spain in the Middle Ages*, 1977.
107 Maltby, W. S., *Alba: A Biography of Fernando Alvarez de Toledo 1507–1582*, Berkeley, Cal., 1983.
108 Maltby, W. S., *The Black Legend in England and the Development of Anti-Spanish Sentiment, 1558–1660*, Durham, NC, 1971.
109 Marañón, G., *Antonio Pérez*, 2 vols, Madrid, 1963.
110 Maravall, J. A., 'Las etapas del pensamiento político de Carlos V', in *Revista de estudios políticos*, 100, Madrid, 1958.

Bibliography

111 Marongiu, A., *Medieval Parliaments*, 1968.
112 Martin, C. and Parker, G., *The Spanish Armada*, 1988.
113 Martz, L., *Poverty and Welfare in Habsburg Spain: The Example of Toledo*, Cambridge, 1983.
114 Matilla Tascón, A., *Historia de las minas de Almadén*, vol. 1: *Desde la época romana hasta el año 1645*, Madrid, 1958.
115 Mattingly, G., *The Defeat of the Spanish Armada*, 1959.
116 Mattingly, G., *Renaissance Diplomacy*, 1955.
117 Merriman, R. B., *The Rise of the Spanish Empire in the Old World and the New*, vol. 4: *Philip the Prudent*, New York, 1934, repr. 1962.
118 Motley, J. L., *History of the United Netherlands*, 4 vols, New York, 1867.
119 Nadal Oller, J., 'La Revolución de los Precios Españoles en el Siglo XVI', *Hispania*, xix, Madrid, 1959.
120 Nader, H., *Liberty in Absolutist Spain. The Habsburg Sale of Towns, 1516–1700*, Baltimore, Md., 1990.
121 Oman, C. W. C., *The Sixteenth Century*, New York, 1937.
122 Pagden, A., *Spanish Imperialism and the Political Imagination*, New Haven, Conn., 1990.
123 Parker, G., *Philip II*, 1979.
124 Parker, G., *The Army of Flanders and the Spanish Road, 1567–1659*, Cambridge, 1972.
125 Parker, G., *The Dutch Revolt*, 2nd edition, 1985.
126 Parker, G., 'Why the Armada Failed', *History Today*, 38, 1988.
127 Parker, G., 'Why did the Dutch Revolt last so long?' in *Spain and the Netherlands, 1559–1659: Ten Studies*, 1979.
128 Parker, G., 'Spain, her enemies and the revolt of the Netherlands, 1559–1648', in *Spain and the Netherlands, 1559–1659: Ten Studies*, 1979.
129 Parker, G., 'The Emergence of Modern Finance in Europe, 1500–1730', in C. M. Cipolla (ed.), *The Fontana Economic History of Europe*, 1974.
130 Parker, G., 'Some Recent Work on the Inquisition in Spain and Italy', *Journal of Modern History*, 54, 1982.
131 Parker, G., *The Military Revolution*, Cambridge, 1988.
132 Parry, J. H., *The Spanish Seaborne Empire*, 1966.
133 Petrie, Sir C., *Philip II*, 1963.
134 Phillips, C. R., *Ciudad Real 1500–1750: Growth, Crisis and Readjustment in the Spanish Economy*, Cambridge, Mass., 1979.
135 Phillips, C. R., 'The Spanish Wool Trade 1500–1780', *Journal of Economic History*, xlii, 1982.

Bibliography

136 Pierson, P., *Philip II of Spain*, 1975.
137 Pierson, P., *Commander of the Armada*, New Haven, Conn., 1989.
138 Pike, R., *Aristocrats and Traders: Sevillian Society in the Sixteenth Century*, Ithaca, NY, 1972.
139 Pike, R., *Enterprise and Adventure: the Genoese in Seville and the Opening of the New World*, Ithaca, NY, 1966.
140 Pinto Crespo, V., *Inquisición y control ideológico en la España del siglo XVI*, Madrid, 1983.
141 Pirenne, H., *Histoire de Belgique*, iii, Brussels, 1923.
142 Pollitt, R., 'John Hawkins' Troublesome Voyages: Merchants, Bureaucrats and the Origins of the Slave Trade', *Journal of British Studies*, 12, 1973,
143 Porreños, B., *Dichos y Lechos del rey Felipe Segundo*, Cuenca, 1621.
144 Potter, D., 'The Duc de Guise and the Fall of Calais, 1557–58', *English Historical Review*, 388, 98, 1983.
145 Rady, M., *The Netherlands: Revolt and Independence 1550–1650* 1987.
146 Randell, K., *The Catholic and Counter Reformations*, 1990.
147 Ranke, L. von, *The Ottoman and the Spanish Empires in the Sixteenth and Seventeenth Centuries*, trans. by W. K. Kelly, 1843.
148 Reitzer, L., 'Some Observations on Castilian Commerce and Finance in the Sixteenth Century', *Journal of Modern History*, xxxii, 1960.
149 Ribalta, P. M., *Consejos y audiencias durante el reinado de Felipe II*, Valladolid, 1984.
150 Ringrose, D. R., 'The Impact of a New Capital City: Madrid, Toledo and New Castile, 1560–1660', *Journal of Economic History*, xiii, 1973.
151 Rodríguez-Salgado, M. J., 'From Spanish Ruler to European Ruler: Philip II and the Creation of an Empire', Hull University Ph.D. thesis, 1984.
152 Rodríguez-Salgado, M. J., (ed.), *The Armada*, 1988.
153 Rodríguez-Salgado, M. J., *The Changing Face of Empire: Charles V, Philip II and Habsburg Authority, 1551–59*, Cambridge, 1988.
154 Ruiz Martín, F., 'Las finanzas españoles durante el reinado de Felipe II', *Cuadernos de Historia*, 2, Madrid, 1968.
155 Ruiz Martín, F., 'La Población española al comienzo de los tiempos modernos', *Cuadernos de Historia*, 1, Madrid, 1967.
156 Ruiz Martín, F., 'Juan y Pau Sauri: Negociantes Catalanes que Intervienen en las Empresas Imperiales de Felipe II', in

Homenaje al Sr. D. Juan Reglà Campistol, i, Valencia, 1975.

157 Rule, J. C. and TePaske, J. J., (eds), *The Character of Philip II*, Boston, 1963.

158 Scarisbrick, J. J., *The Jesuits and the Catholic Reformation*, Historical Association, New Appreciations in History, 9, 1988.

159 Stradling, R. A., *Europe and the Decline of Spain: A Study of the Spanish System, 1580–1720*, 1981.

160 Sutherland, N. M., *The Massacre of St Bartholomew and the European Conflict, 1559–1572*, 1973.

161 Sutherland, N. M., 'The Foreign Policy of Queen Elizabeth, the Sea Beggars and the Capture of Brill, 1572', in *Princes, Politics and Religion, 1547–1589*, 1984.

162 Swart, K. W., *William the Silent and the Revolt of the Netherlands*, Historical Association, General Series, 94, 1978.

163 Swart, K. W., 'The Black Legend during the Eighty Years' War', in J. S. Bromley and E. H. Kossmann (eds), *Britain and the Netherlands*, vol. v, The Hague, 1975.

164 Thompson, I. A. A., *War and Government in Habsburg Spain, 1560 1620*, 1976.

165 Thompson, I. A. A., 'Crown and Cortes in Castile, 1590–1665', in *Parliaments, Estates and Representation*, vol. 2, no. 1, 1982.

166 Thompson, I. A. A., 'The appointment of the Duke of Medina Sidonia to Command the Spanish Armada', *Historical Journal*, xii, 1969.

167 Thompson, I. A .A., 'The Armada and Administrative Reform: the Spanish Council of War in the Reign of Philip II', *English Historical Review*, 82, 1967.

168 Trevor-Roper, H. R., *Princes and Artists: Patronage and Ideology at Four Habsburg Courts, 1517–1633*, 1976.

169 Truman, R. W. and Kinder, A. Gordon, 'The Pursuit of Spanish Heretics in the Low Countries: the Activities of Alonso del Canto, 1561–64', *Journal of Ecclesiastical History*, 30, 1979.

170 Ulloa, M., *La hacienda real de Castilla en el reinado de Felipe II*, 2nd edition, Madrid, 1977.

171 Ulloa, M., 'Castilian seigniorage and coinage in the reign of Philip II', *Journal of European Economic History*, 4, 1975.

172 Usherwood, S., (ed.), *The Great Enterprise*, 1982.

173 Vassberg, D. E., *Land and Society in Golden Age Castile*, Cambridge, 1984.

174 Viçens Vives, J., 'The Administrative Structure of the State

in the Sixteenth and Seventeenth Centuries', in H. J. Cohn (ed.), *Government in Reformation Europe*, 1971.
175 Viçens Vives, J., *An Economic History of Spain*, New York, 1959.
176 Vilar, P., 'The Problems of the Formation of Capitalism', *Past and Present*, 10, 1956.
177 Vilar, P., *La Catalogne dans l'Espagne Moderne*, vol. 1, Paris, 1962.
178 Villari, R., 'Naples: The Insurrection in Naples of 1585', in E. Cochrane (ed.), *The Late Italian Renaissance*, 1970.
179 Watson, R., *The History of the Reign of Philip the Second, King of Spain*, 3 vols, 1794.
180 Wells, G. E., 'Antwerp and the Government of Philip II, 1555–1567', Cornell University Ph.D. thesis, 1982.
181 Wernham, R. B., *Before the Armada: The Growth of English Foreign Policy, 1485–1588*, 1966.
182 Wernham, R. B., *The Making of Elizabethan Foreign Policy*, Berkeley, Cal., 1980.
183 Wernham, R. B., 'English Policy and the Revolt of the Netherlands', in J. S. Bromley and E. H. Kossmann (eds.), *Britain and the Netherlands: Papers Delivered at the First Anglo-Dutch Historical Conference*, The Hague, 1960.
184 Wilson, C., *Queen Elizabeth and the Revolt of the Netherlands*, 1970.
185 Woltjer, J. T., 'Dutch Privileges, Real and Imaginary', in J. S. Bromley and E. H. Kossmann (eds), *Britain and the Netherlands*, v, The Hague, 1975.
186 Wright, L. P., 'The Military Orders in Sixteenth and Seventeenth Century Spanish Society', *Past and Present*, 43, 1969.
187 Yahya, D., *Morocco in the Sixteenth Century*, 1981.

Index

Index